Real World
Colouring Book
For Advanced Users & Adults

50 Images

**Created From Real Life Photos
For You To Colour As You Please.**

ISBN 978-0-359-97207-4
90000
9 780359 972074

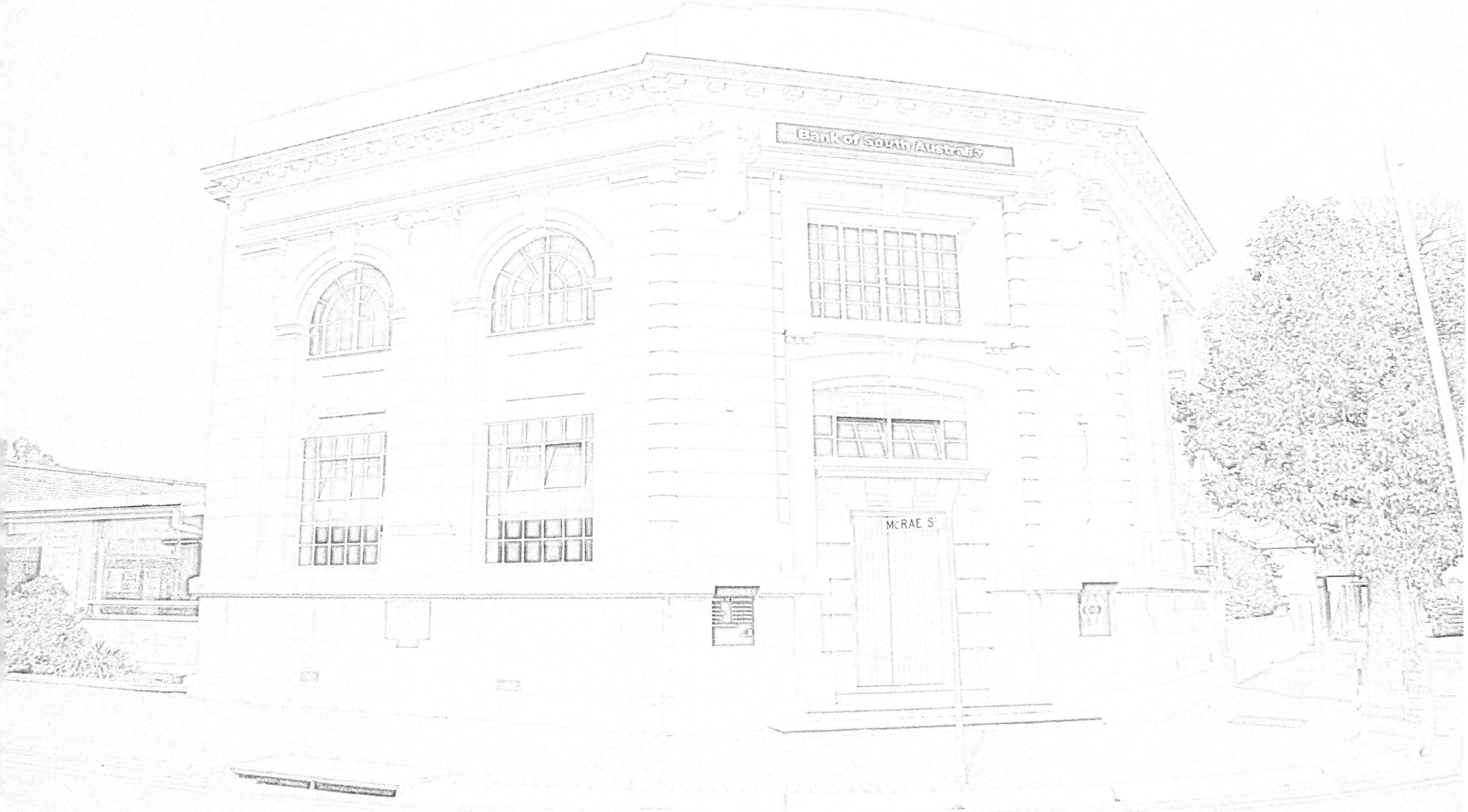
Bank of South Australia
McRAE St

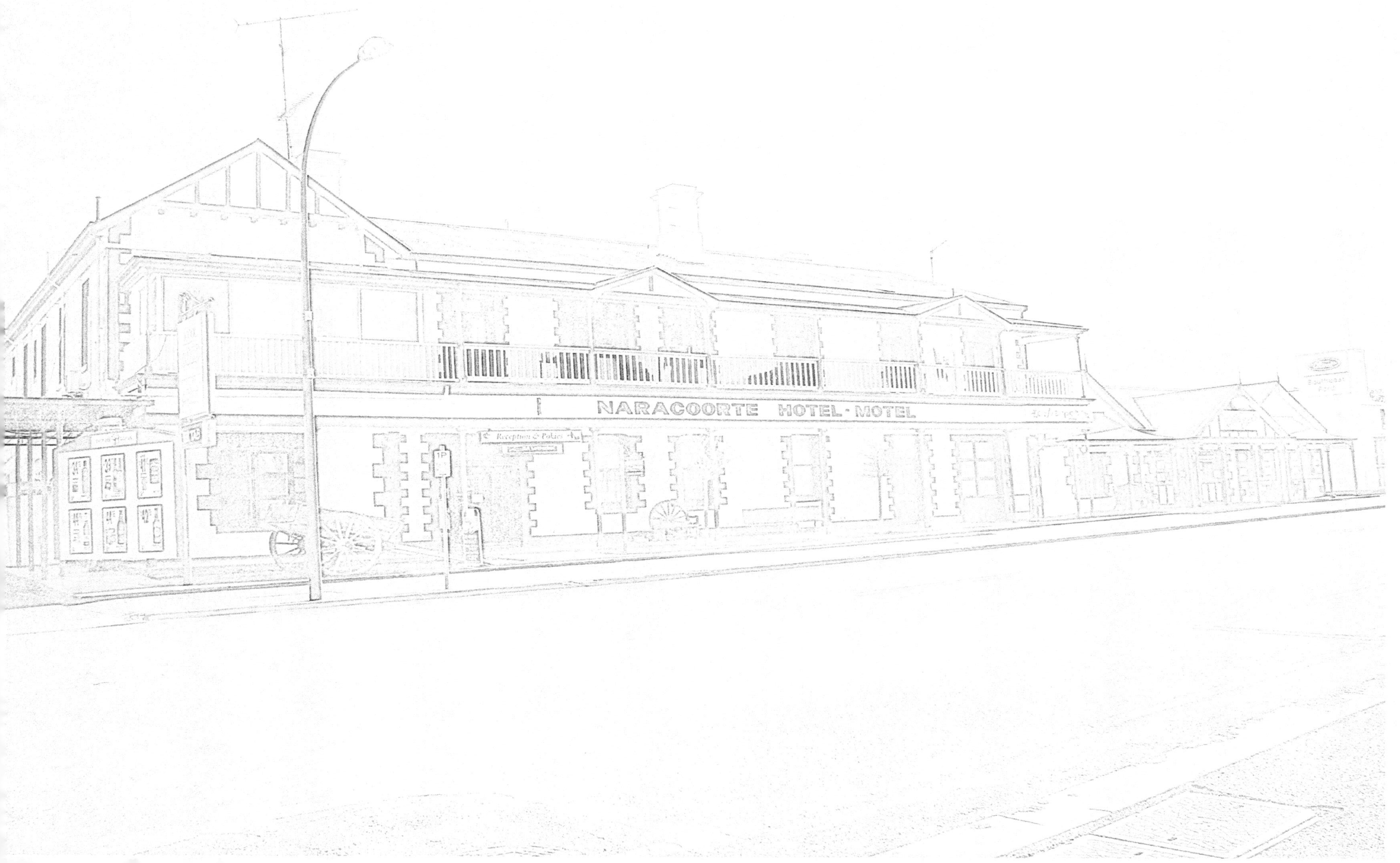
NARACOORTE HOTEL-MOTEL
Reception & Pokies
1P

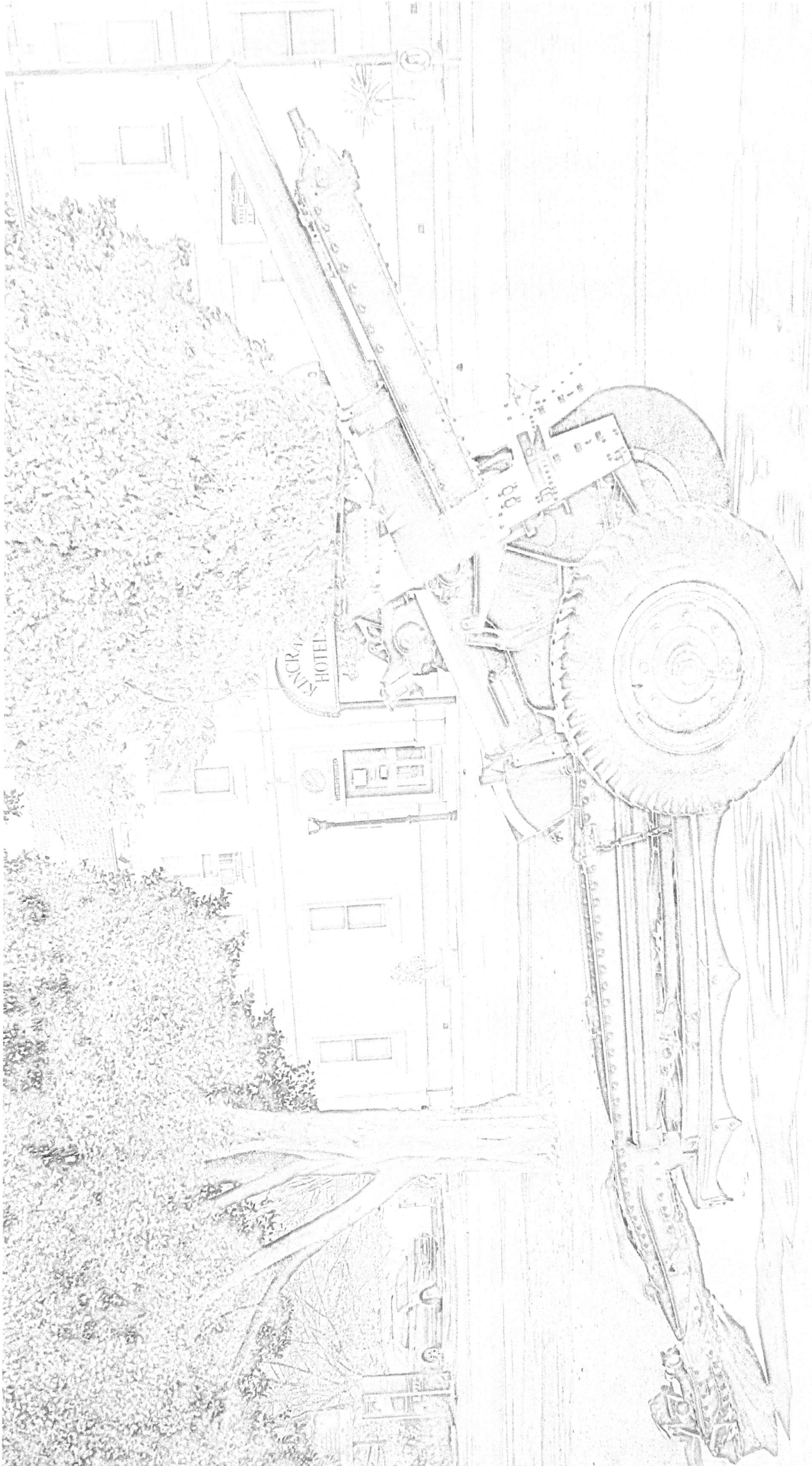
HOTEL

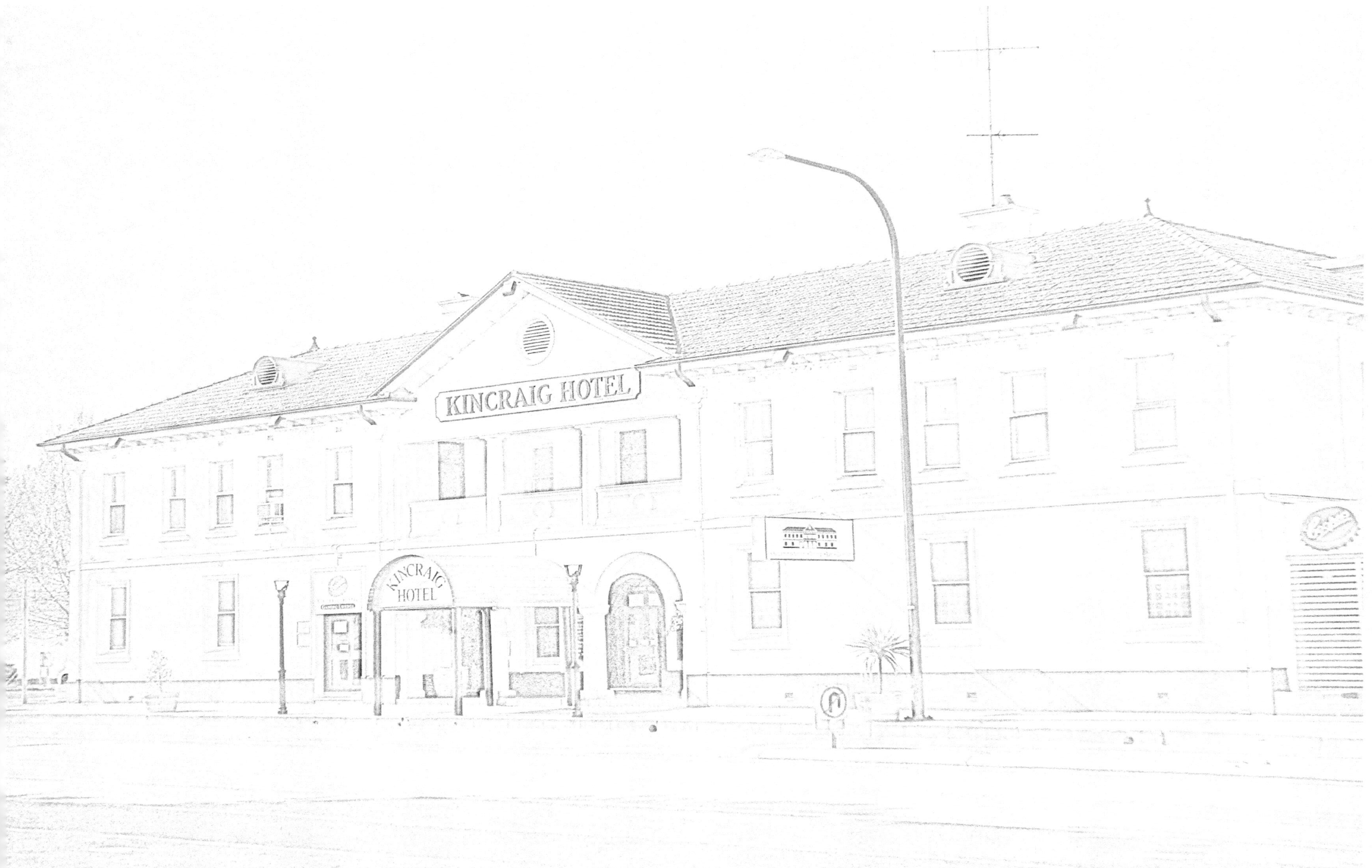
KINCRAIG HOTEL
KINCRAIG
HOTEL

DISTRICT COUNCIL OF NARACOORTE
DE GARIS P
LIBRARY

TAB
BAR

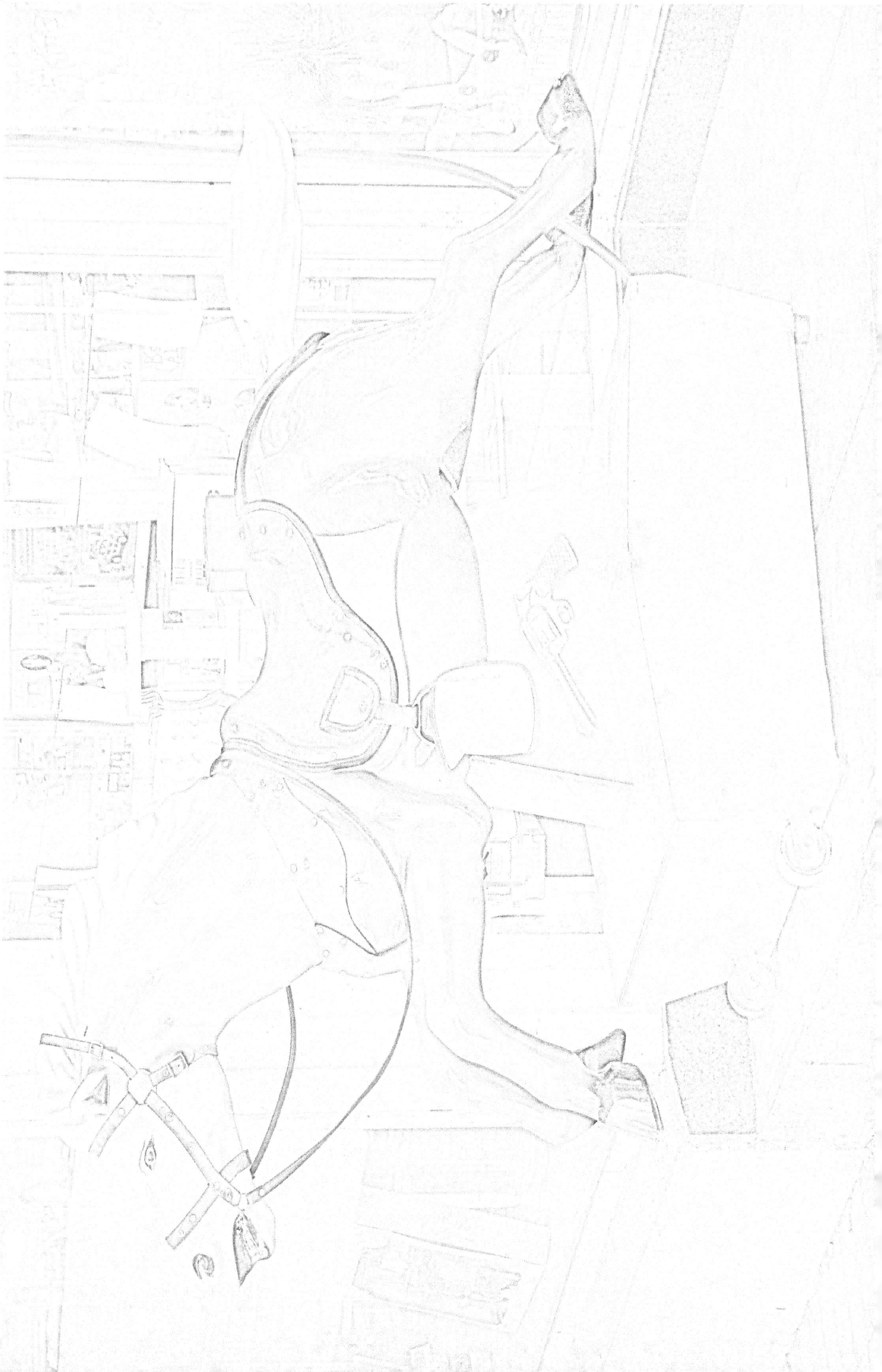

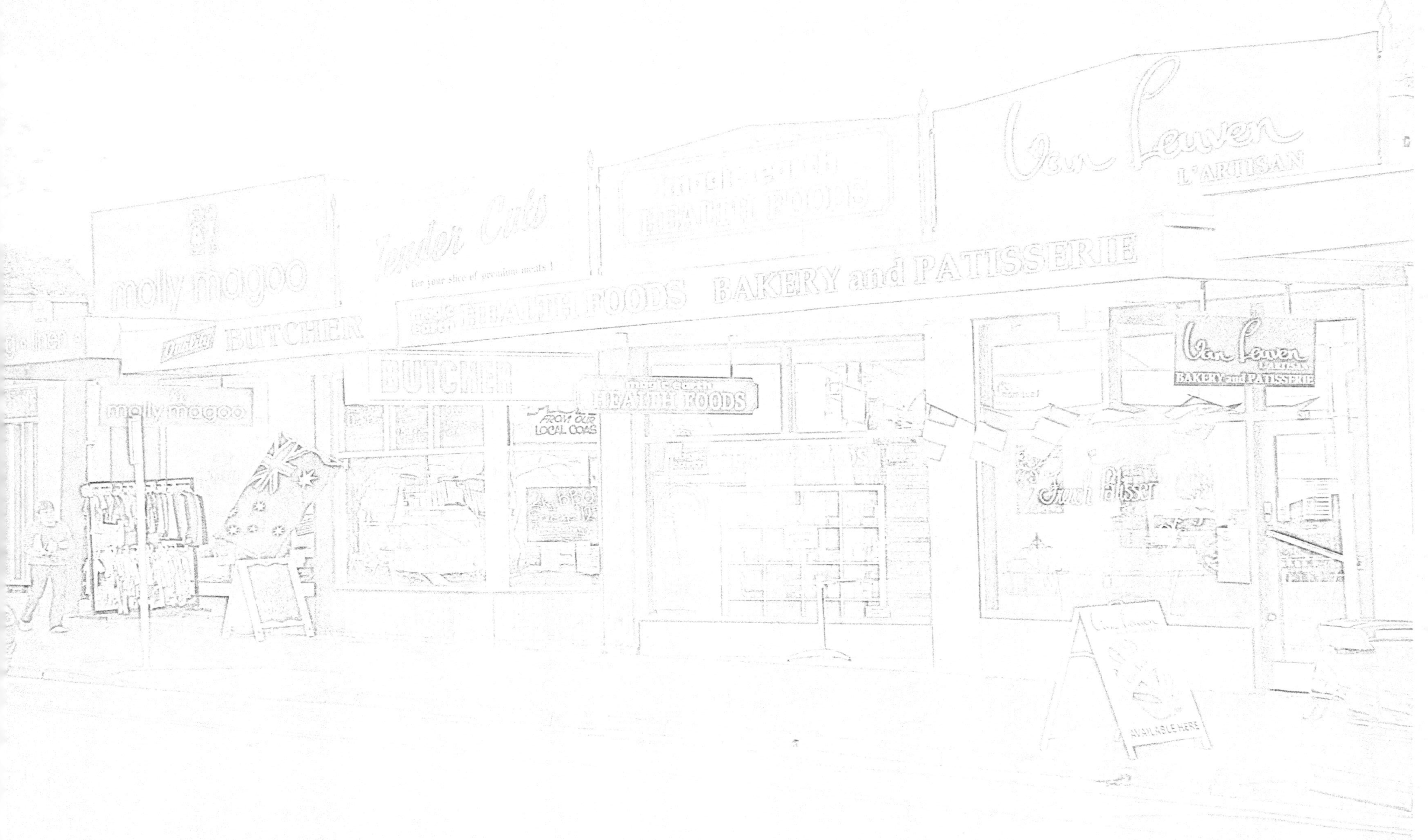

molly mogoo
Tender Cuts
For your slice of premium meats !
Van Leuwen
L'ARTISAN
BUTCHER
HEALTH FOODS
BAKERY and PATISSERIE
molly mogoo
BUTCHER
FROM OUR LOCAL COAS
HEALTH FOODS
Van Leuwen
BAKERY and PATISSERIE
AVAILABLE HERE

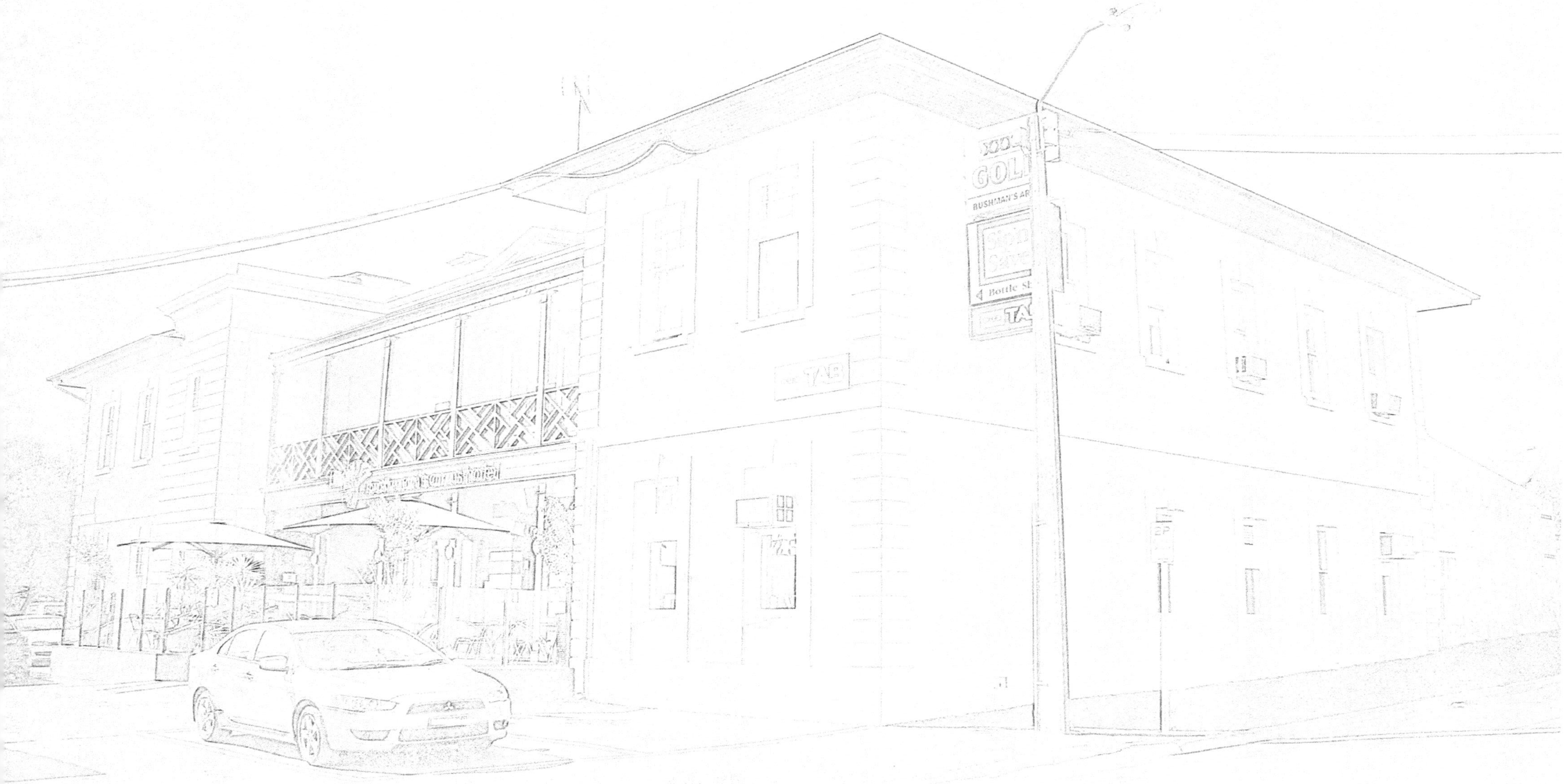
TAB

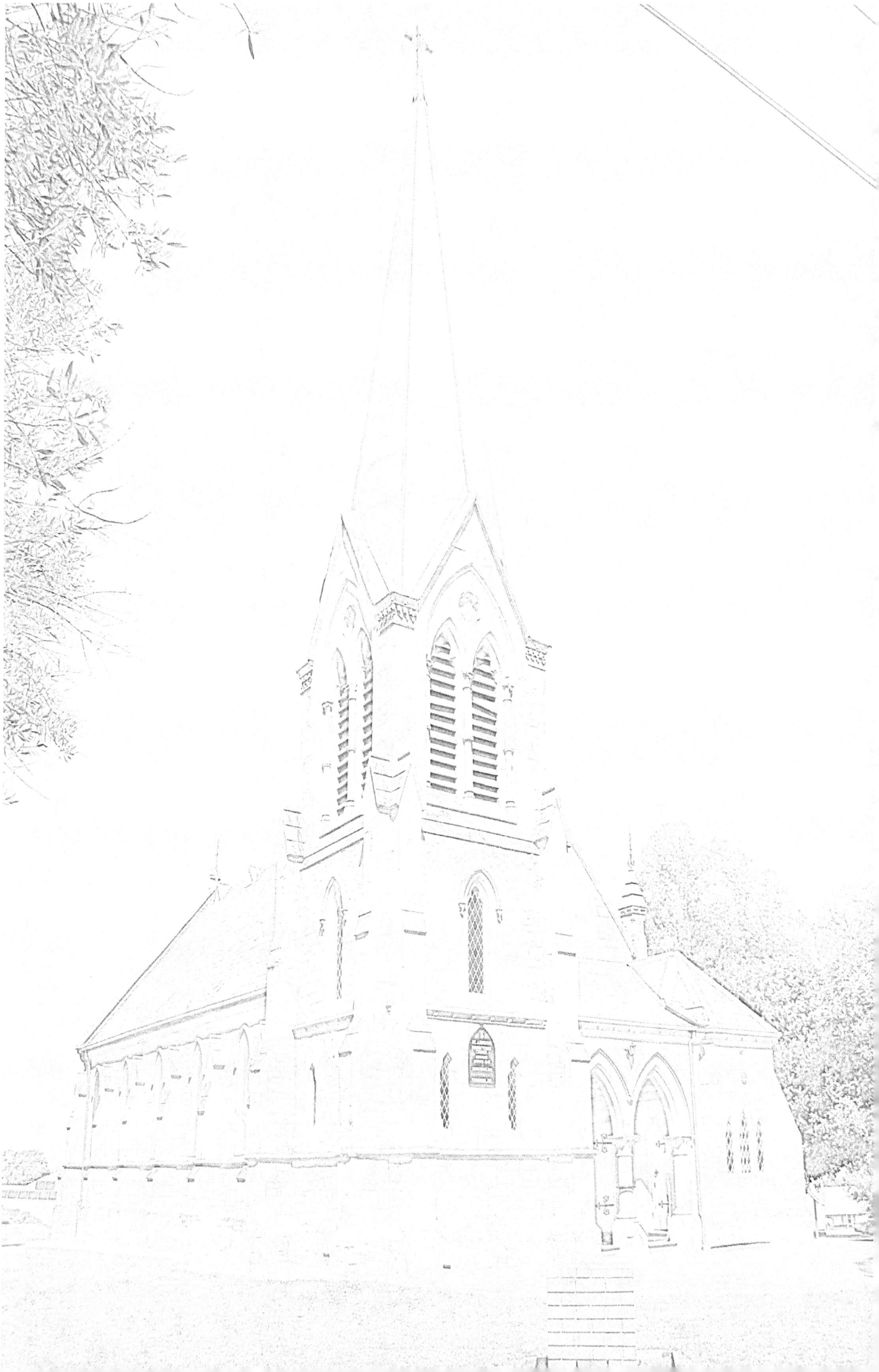

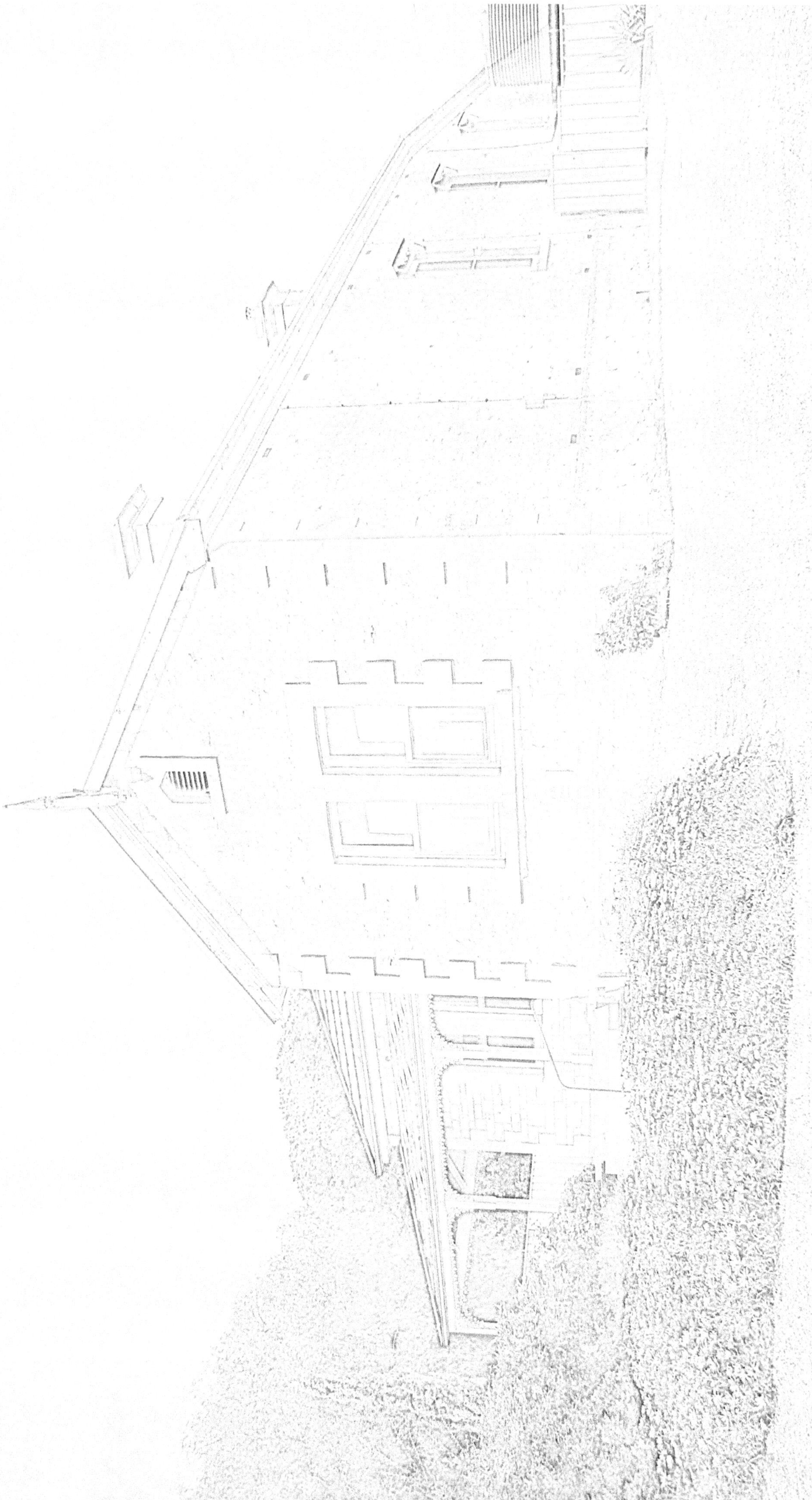

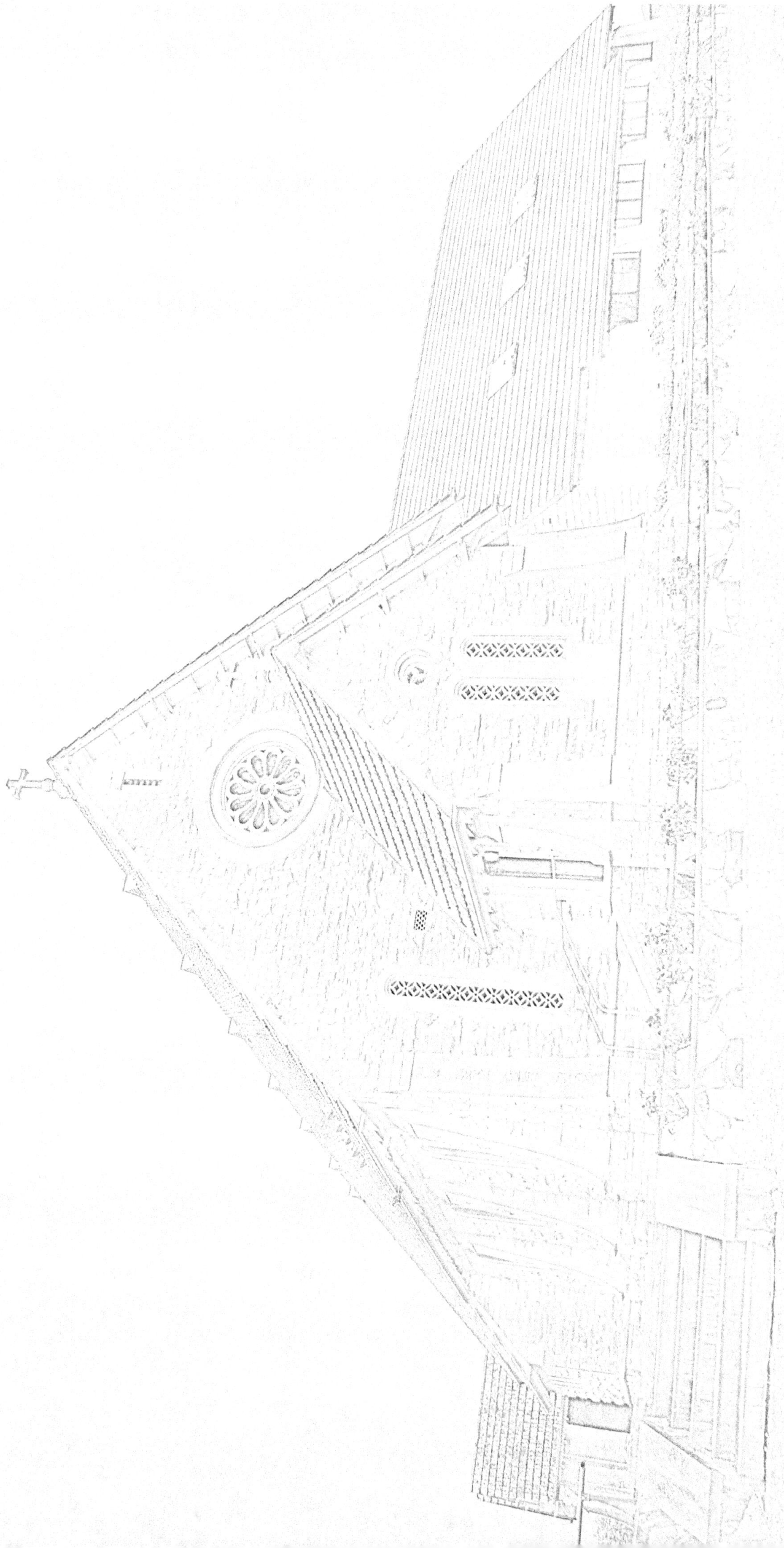

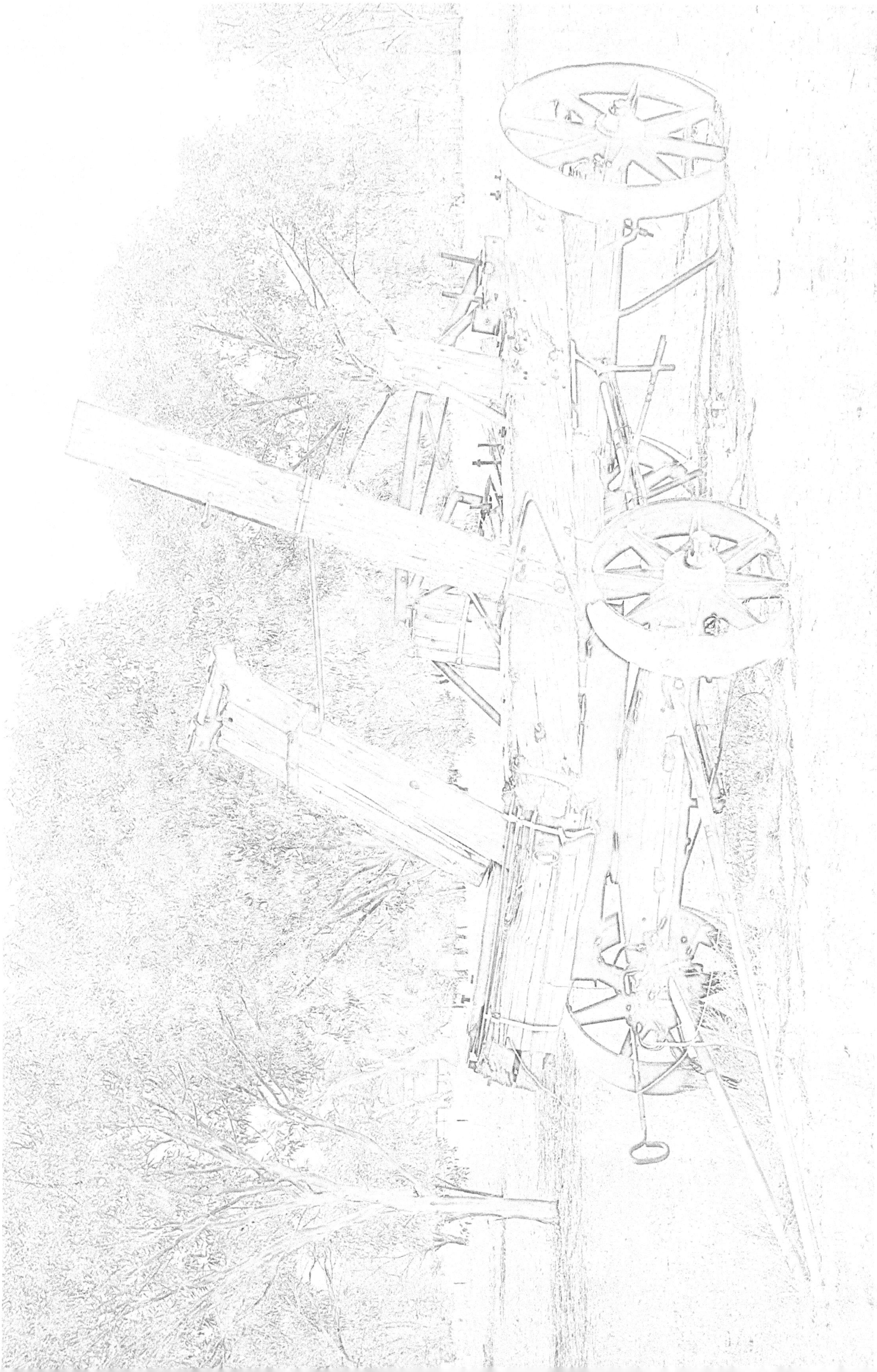

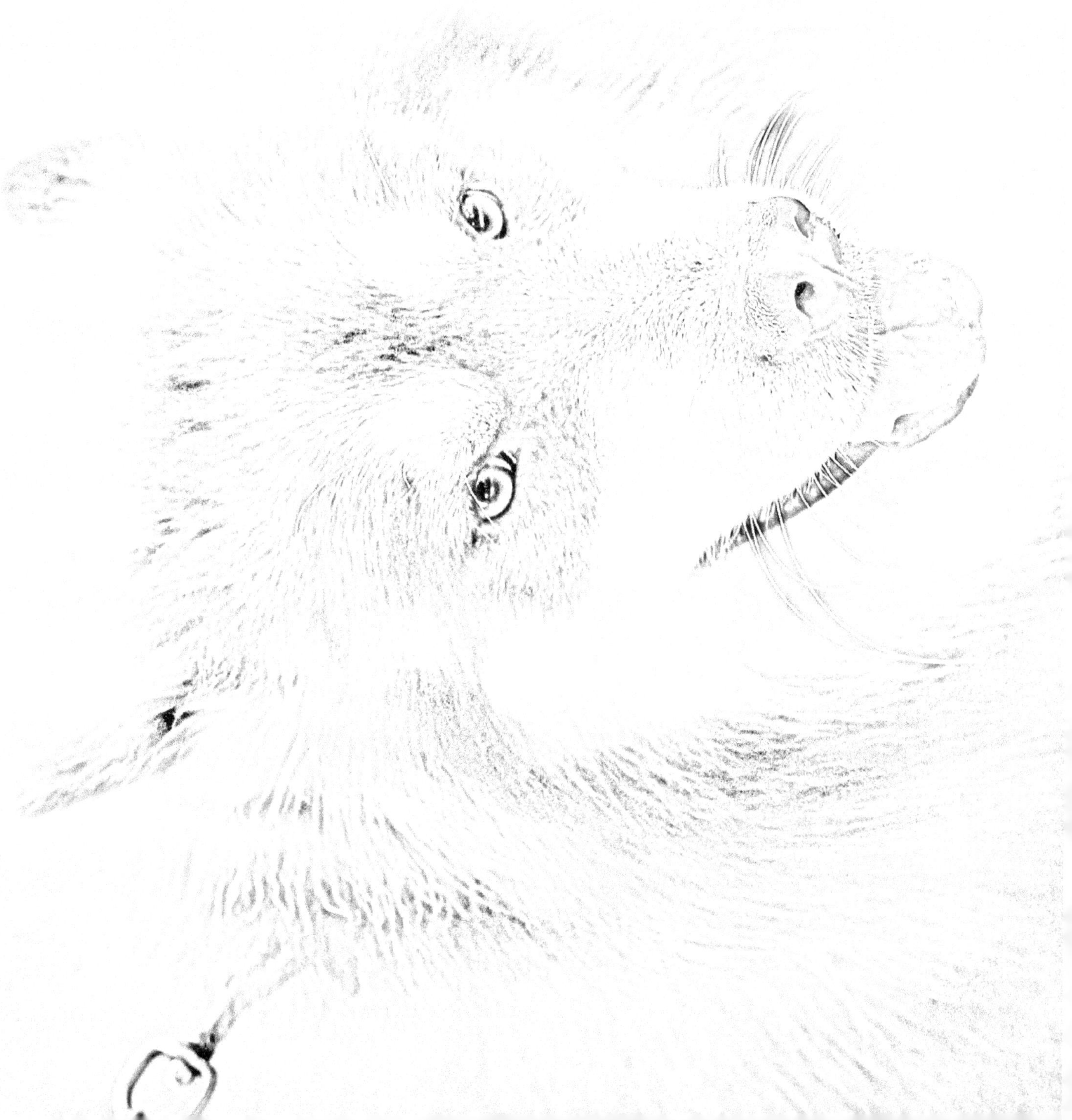

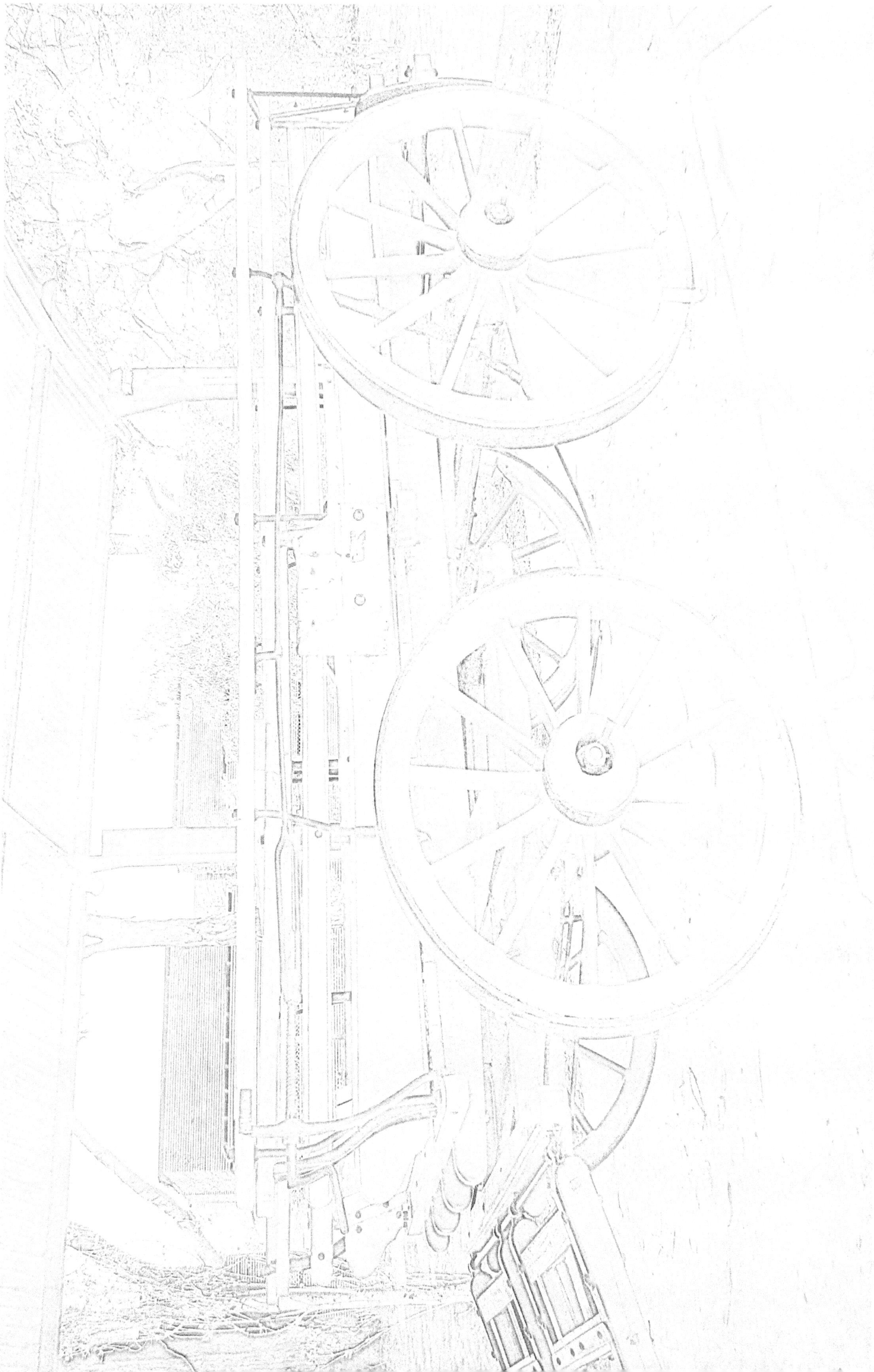

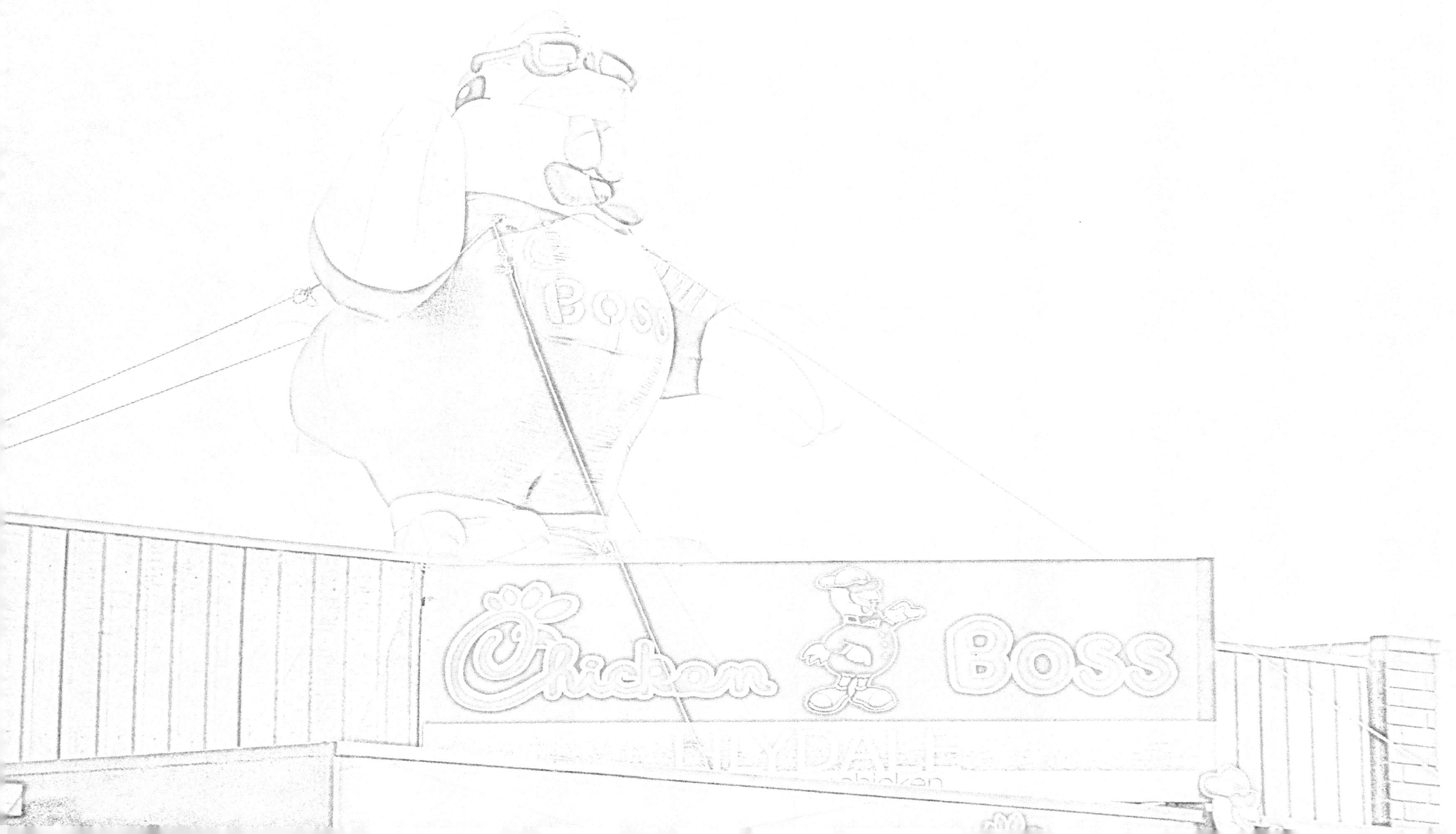
Boss
Chicken
Boss

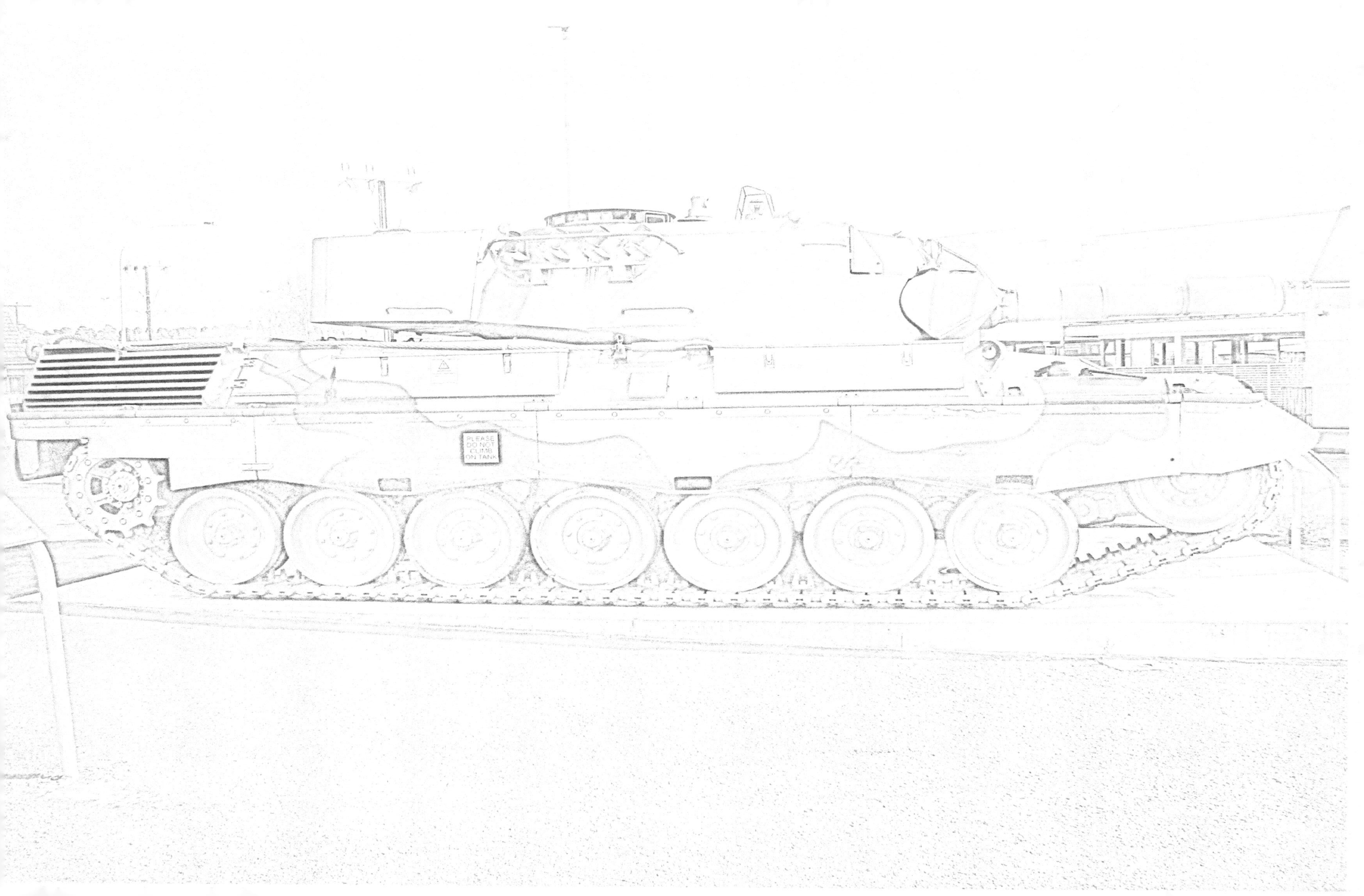
PLEASE
DO NOT
CLIMB
ON TANK

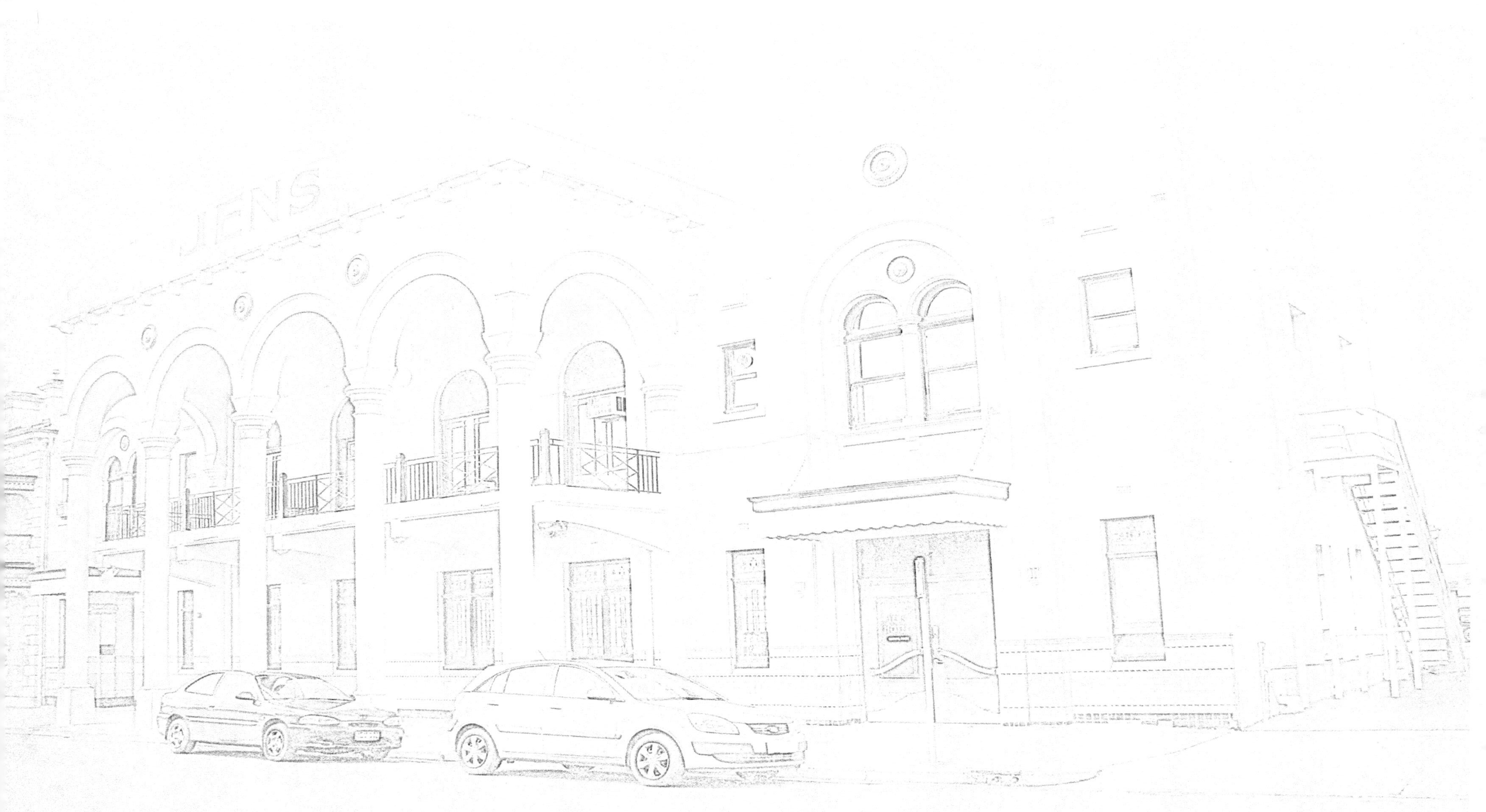

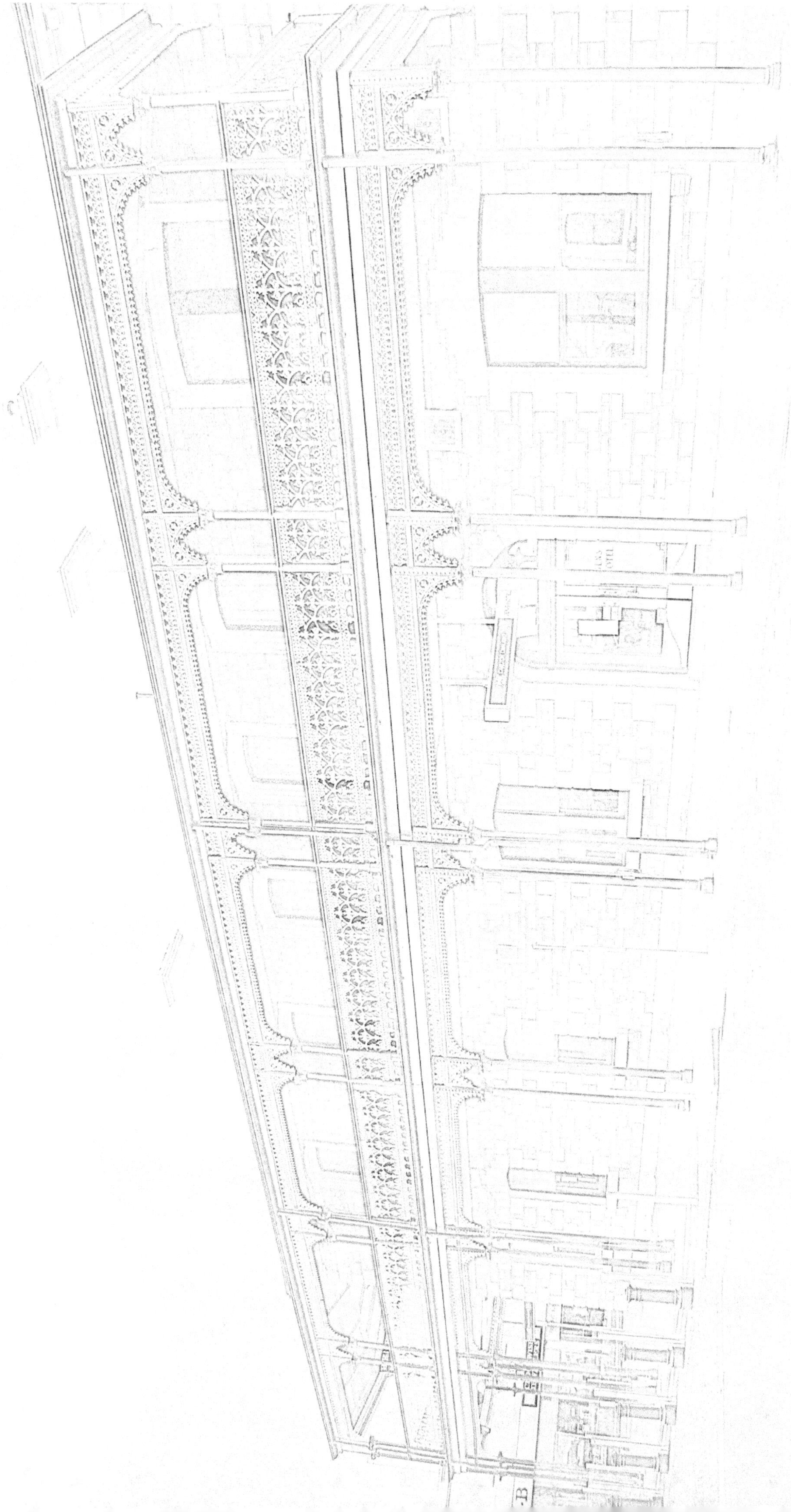

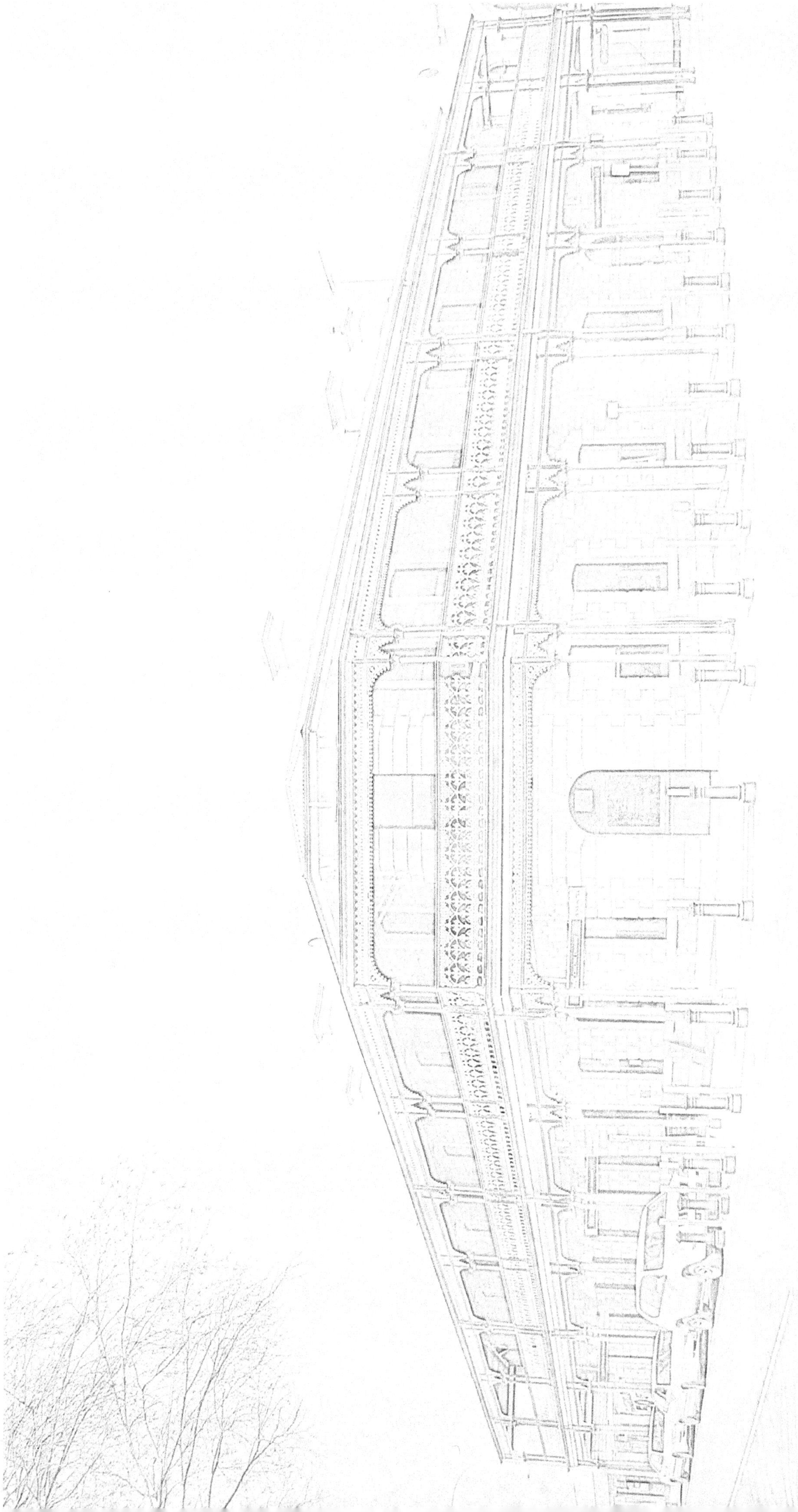

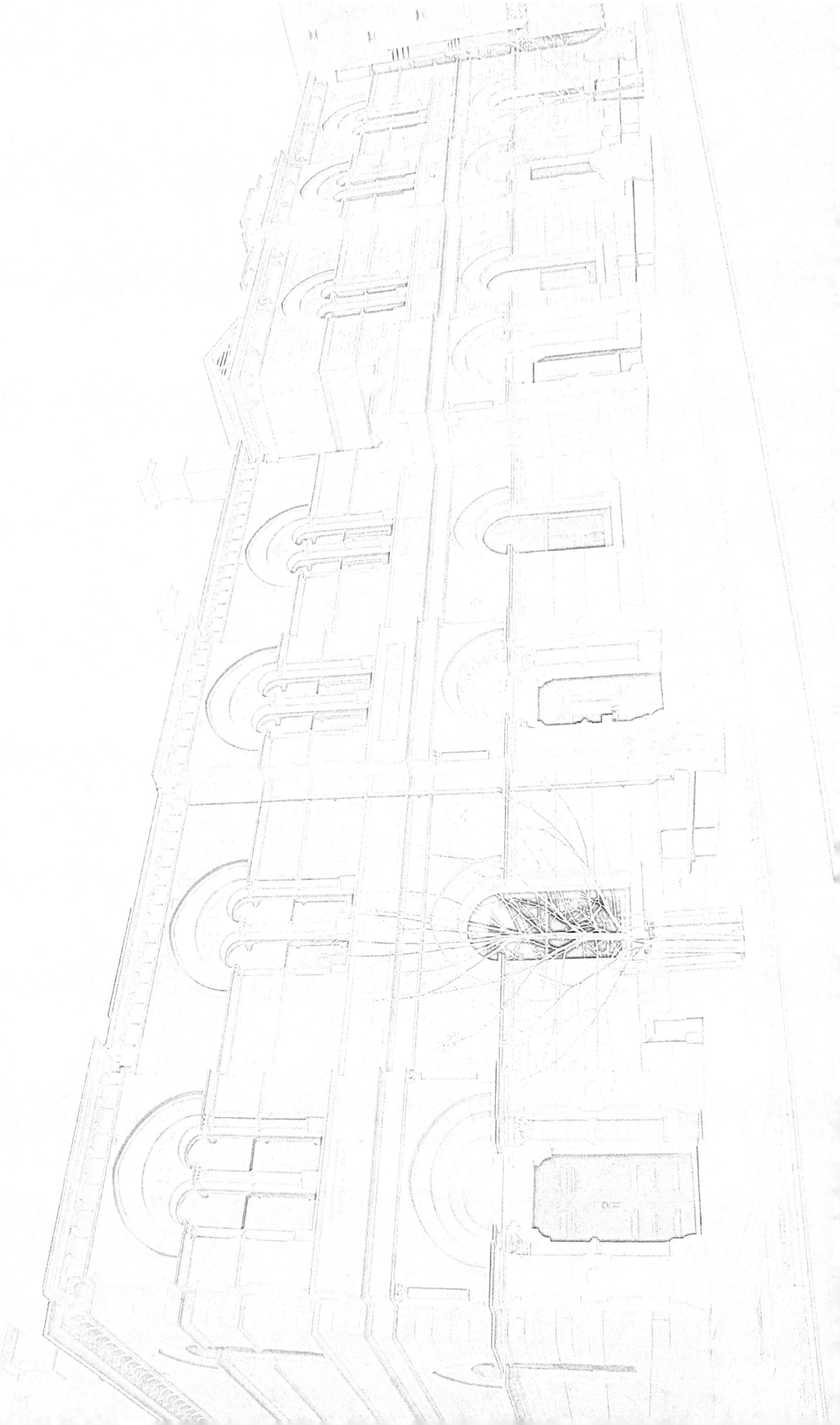

MOUNT
GAMBIER
HOTEL

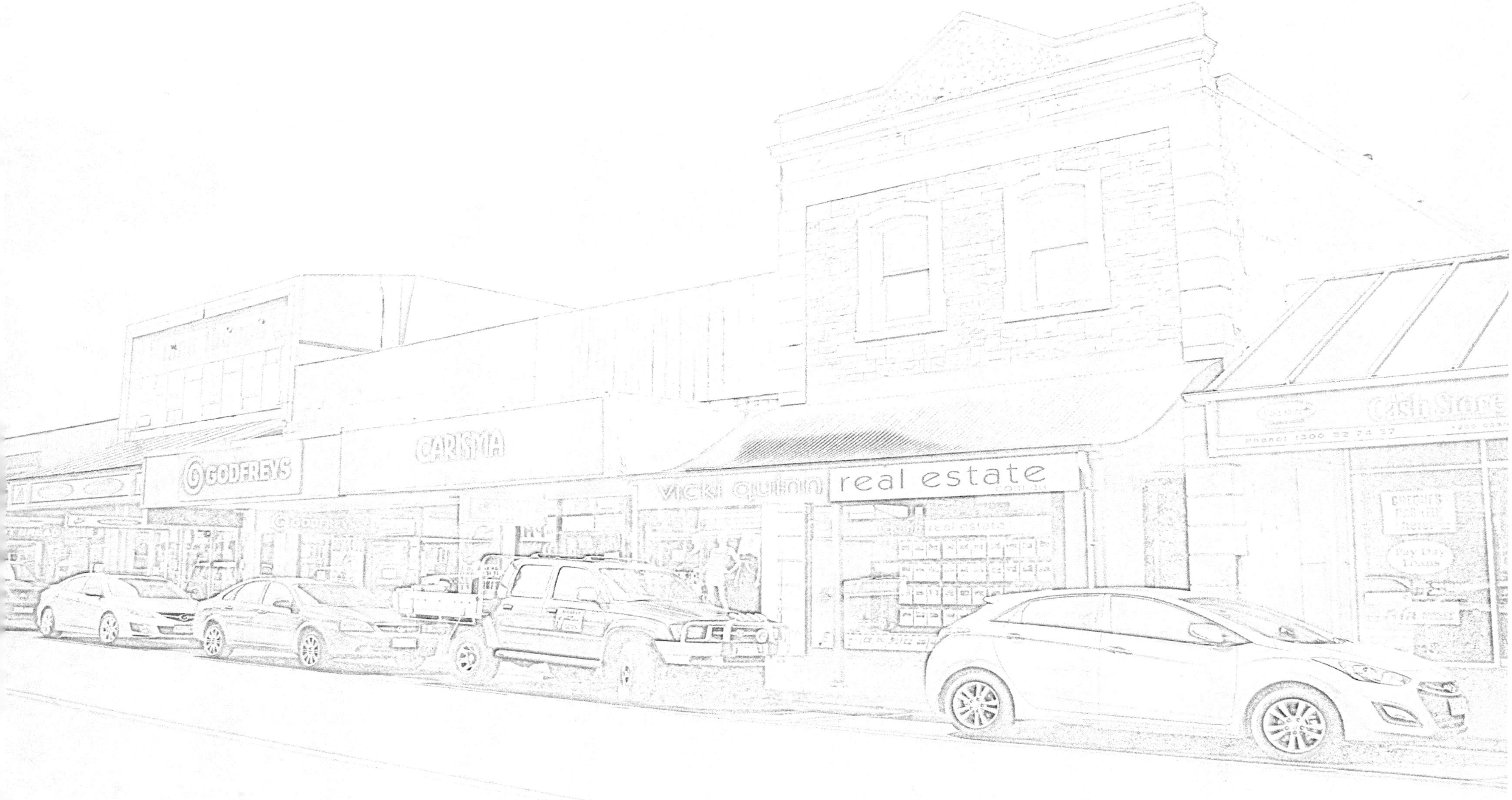
GODFREYS
CARISMA
vicki quinn
real estate
Cash Stores
Phone: 1300 22 74 37
CHEQUES CASHED HERE!
Pay Day Loans

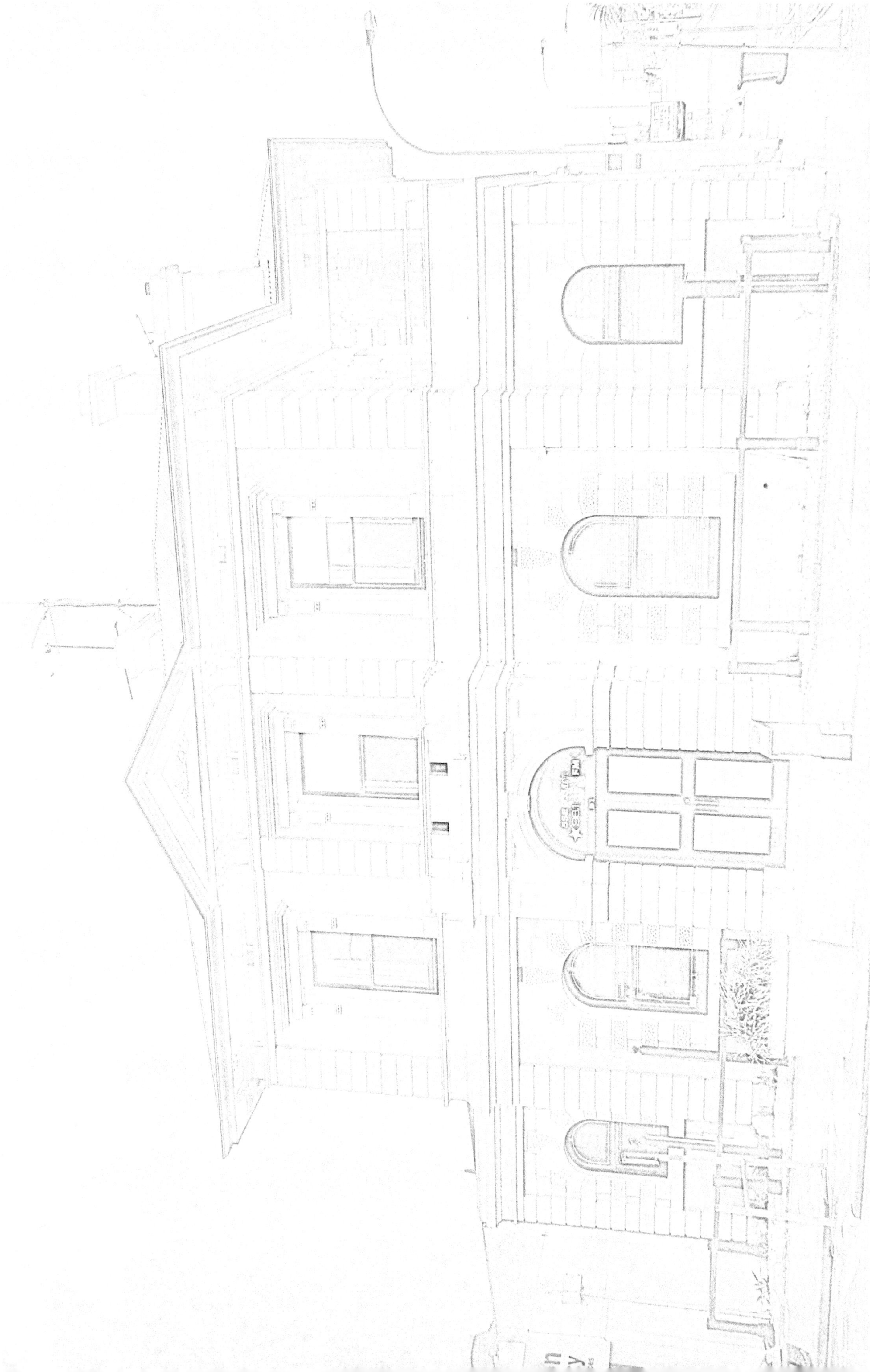

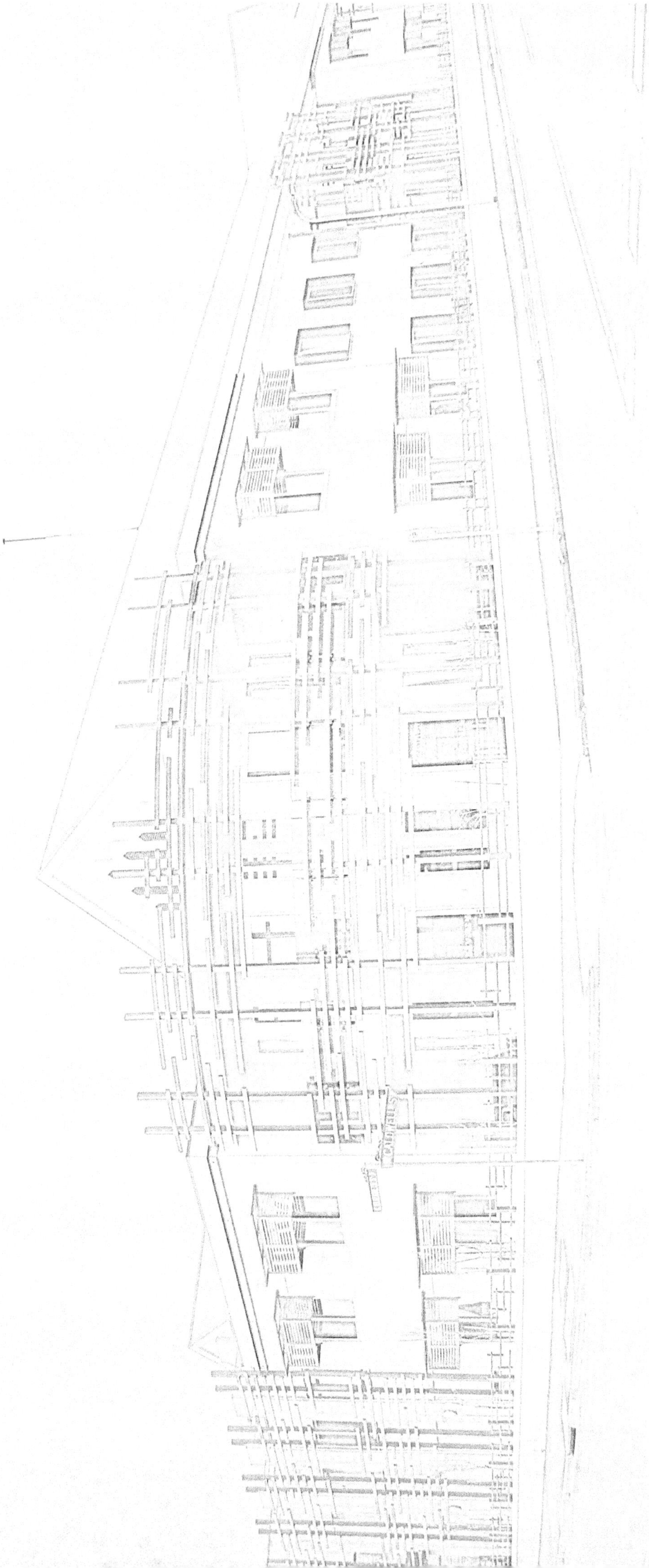

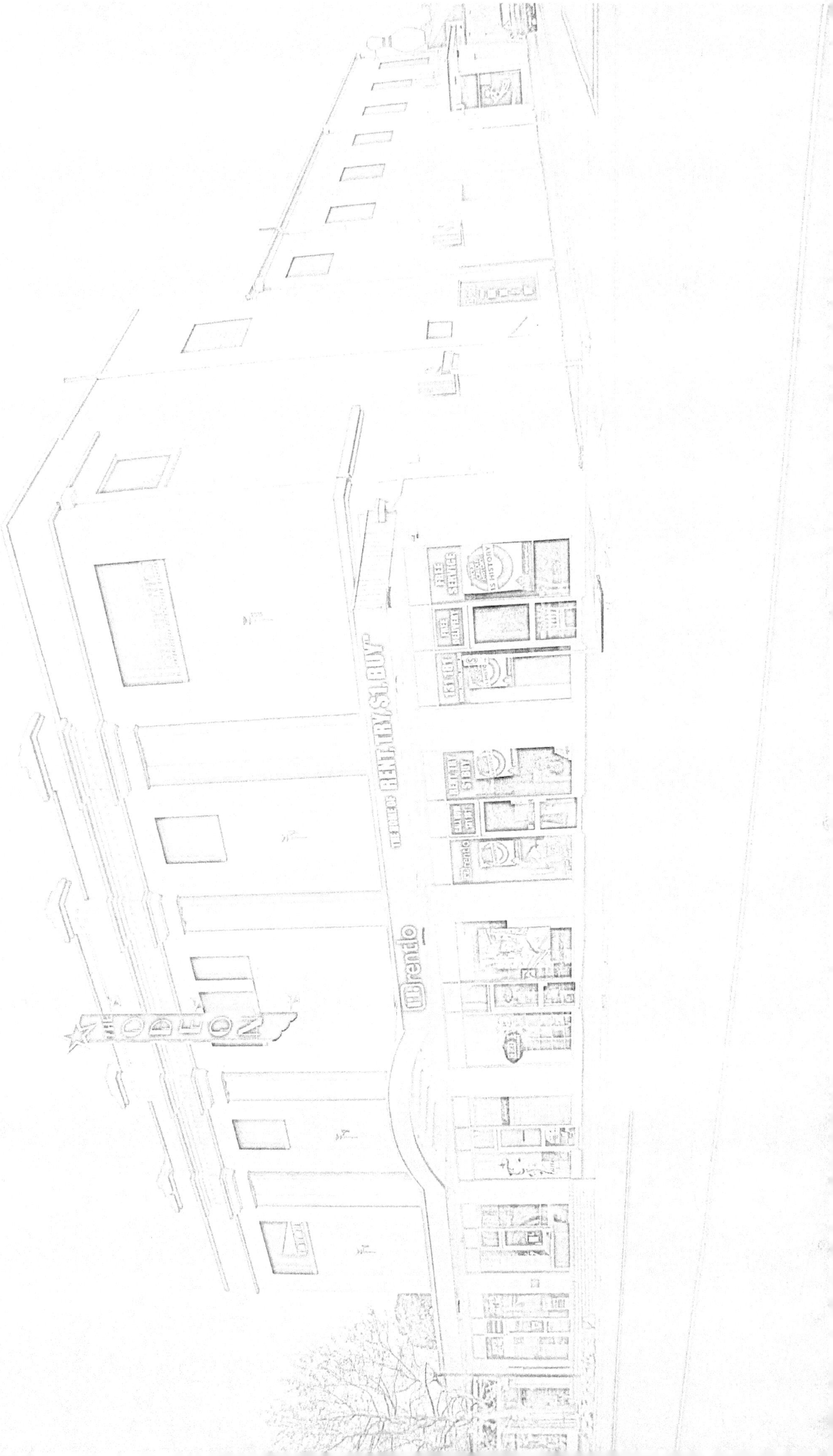

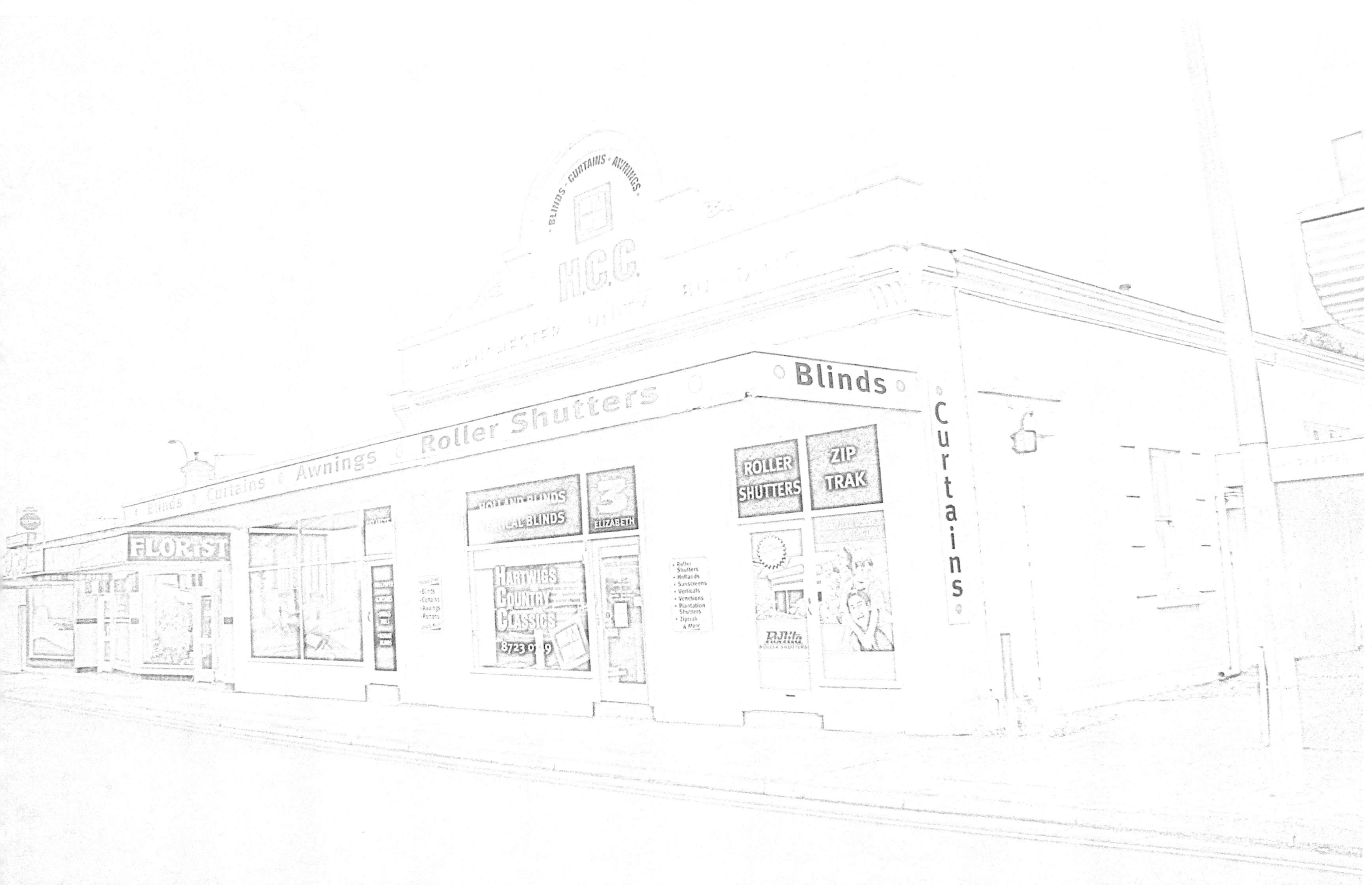

BLINDS · CURTAINS · AWNINGS
H.C.C.
Blinds · Curtains · Awnings · Roller Shutters · Blinds
Curtains
ROLLER SHUTTERS
ZIP TRAK
ELIZABETH
HARTWIGS COUNTRY CLASSICS
FLORIST

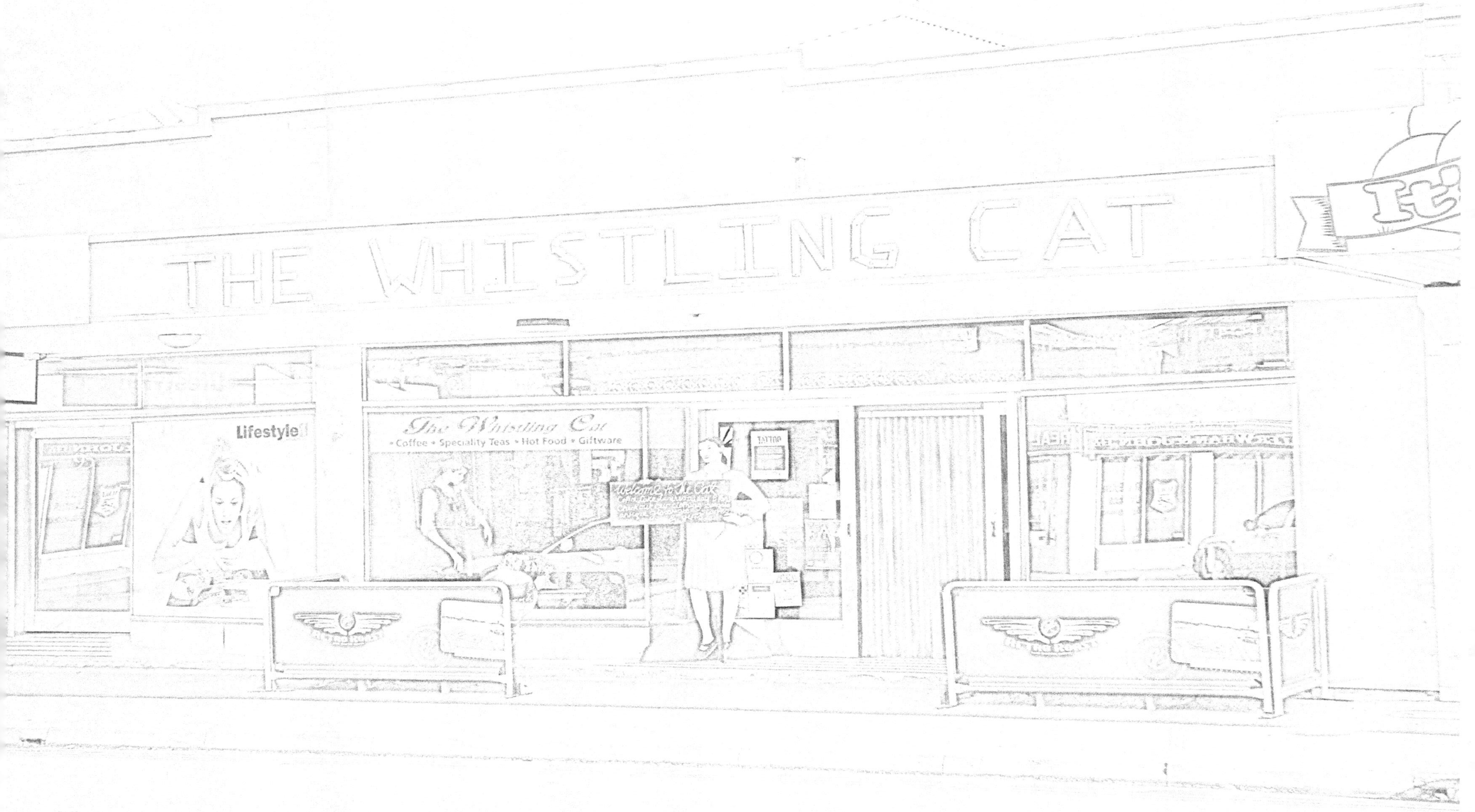
THE WHISTLING CAT
The Whistling Cat
• Coffee • Speciality Teas • Hot Food • Giftware
Lifestyle
TATTOO

19
DeGaris

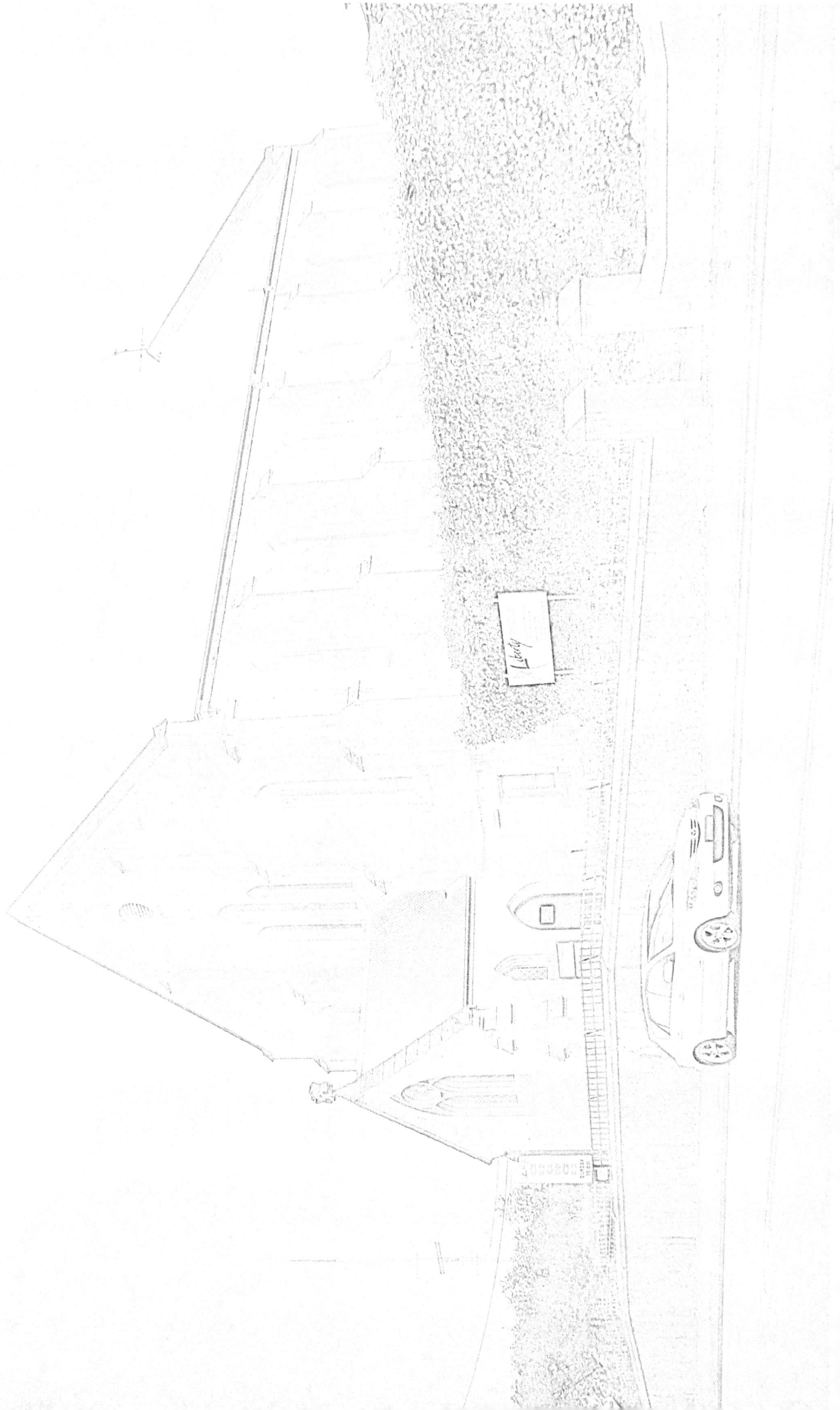

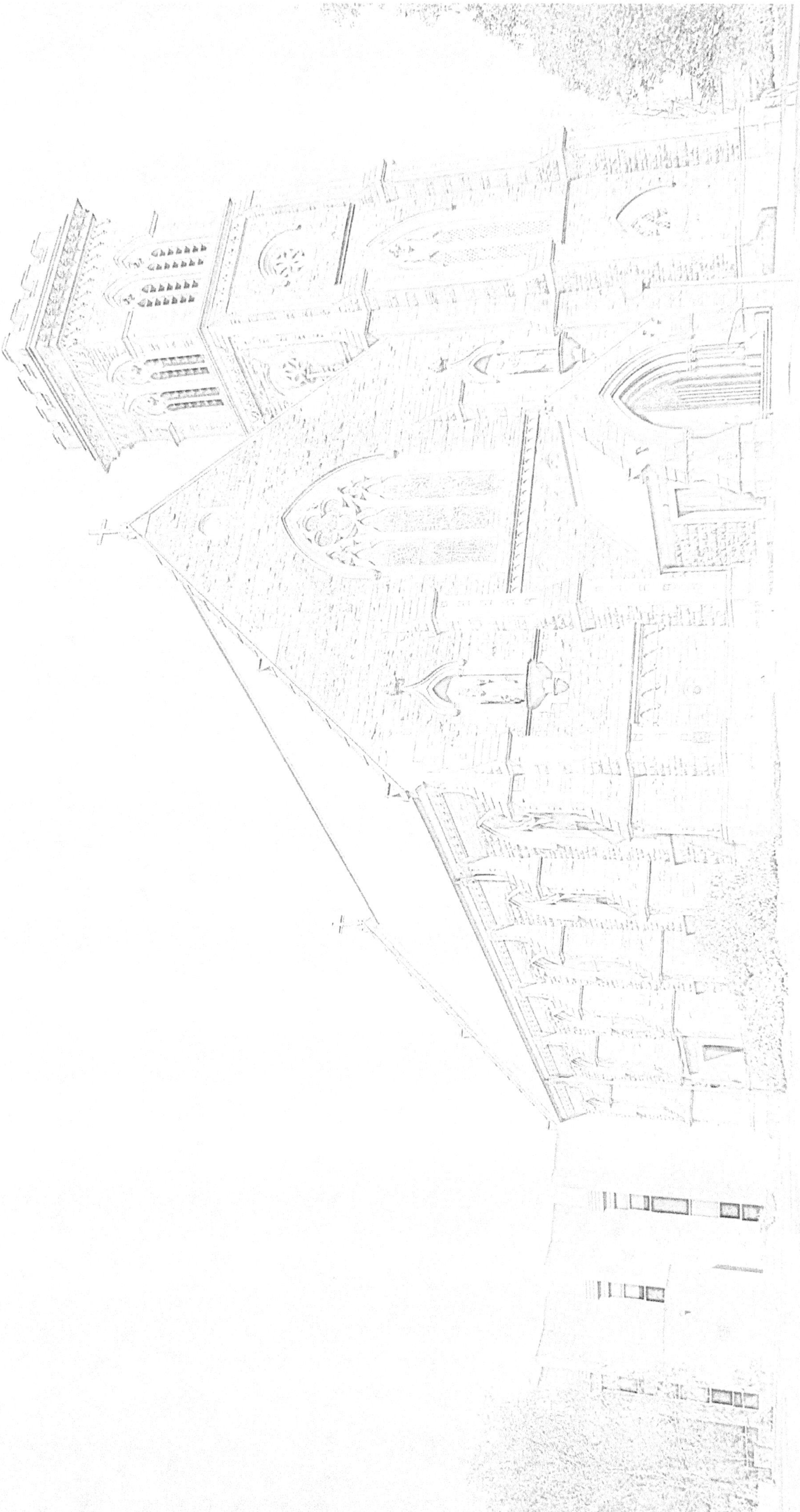

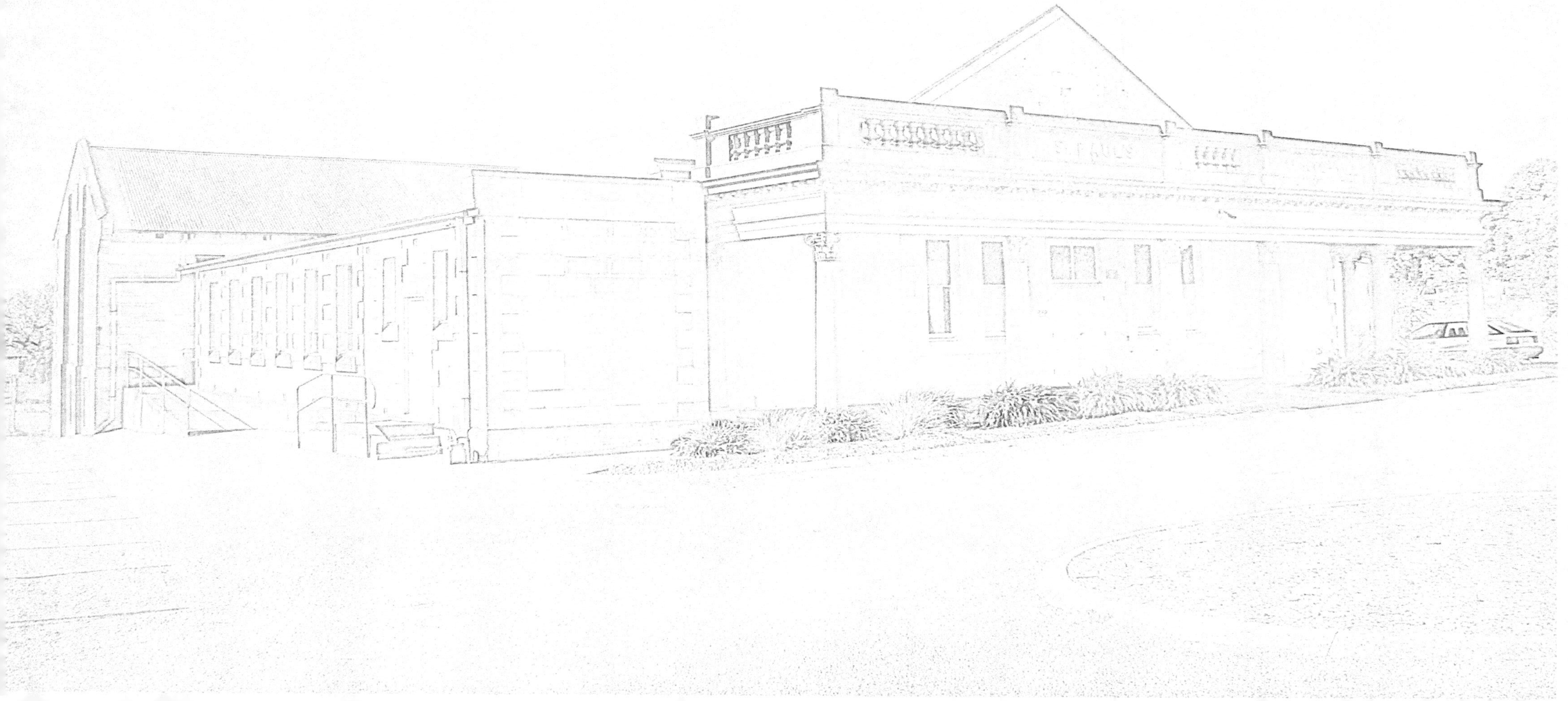

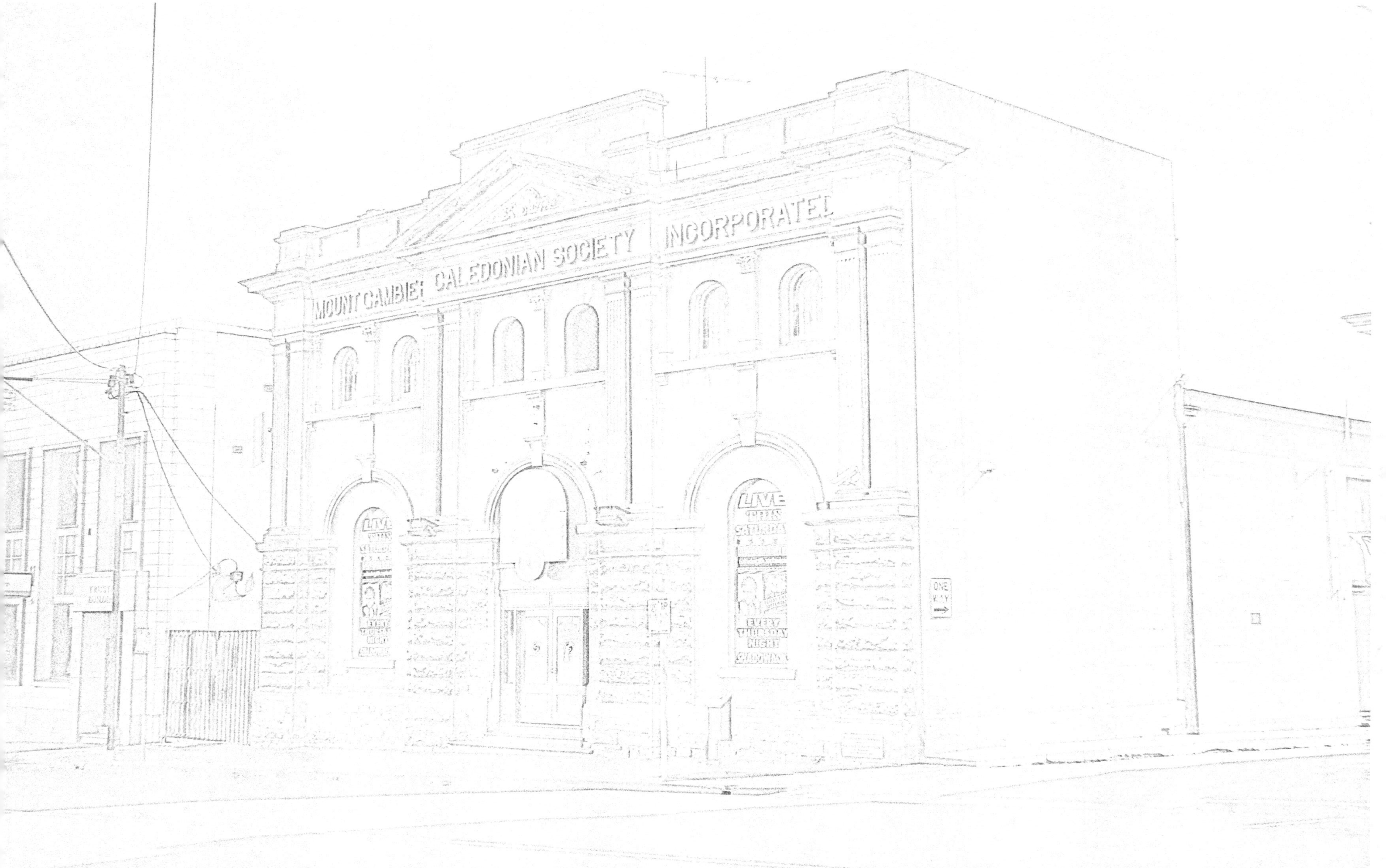

MOUNT GAMBIER CALEDONIAN SOCIETY INCORPORATED
LIVE
SATURDAY
EVERY THURSDAY NIGHT
ONE WAY

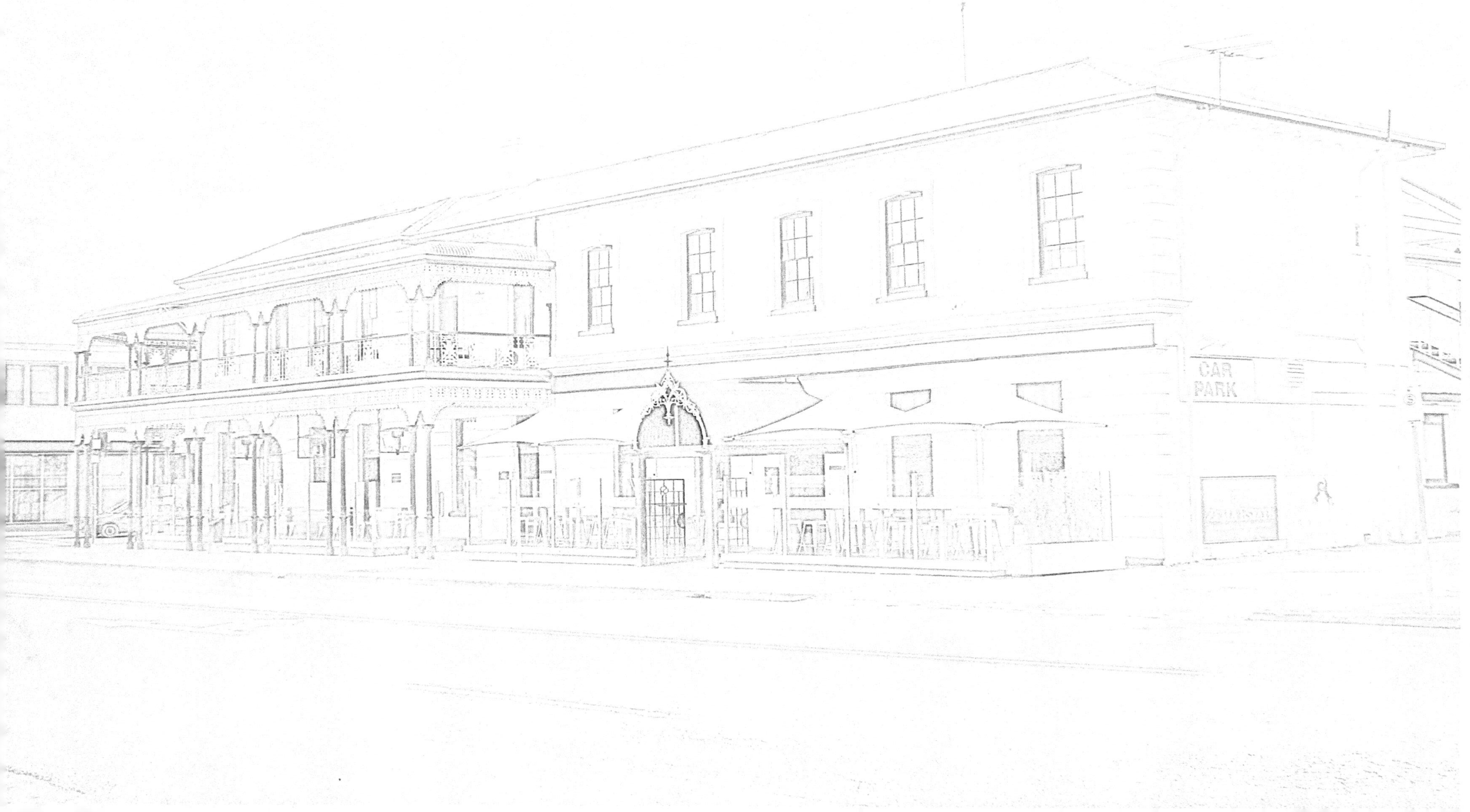
CAR
PARK

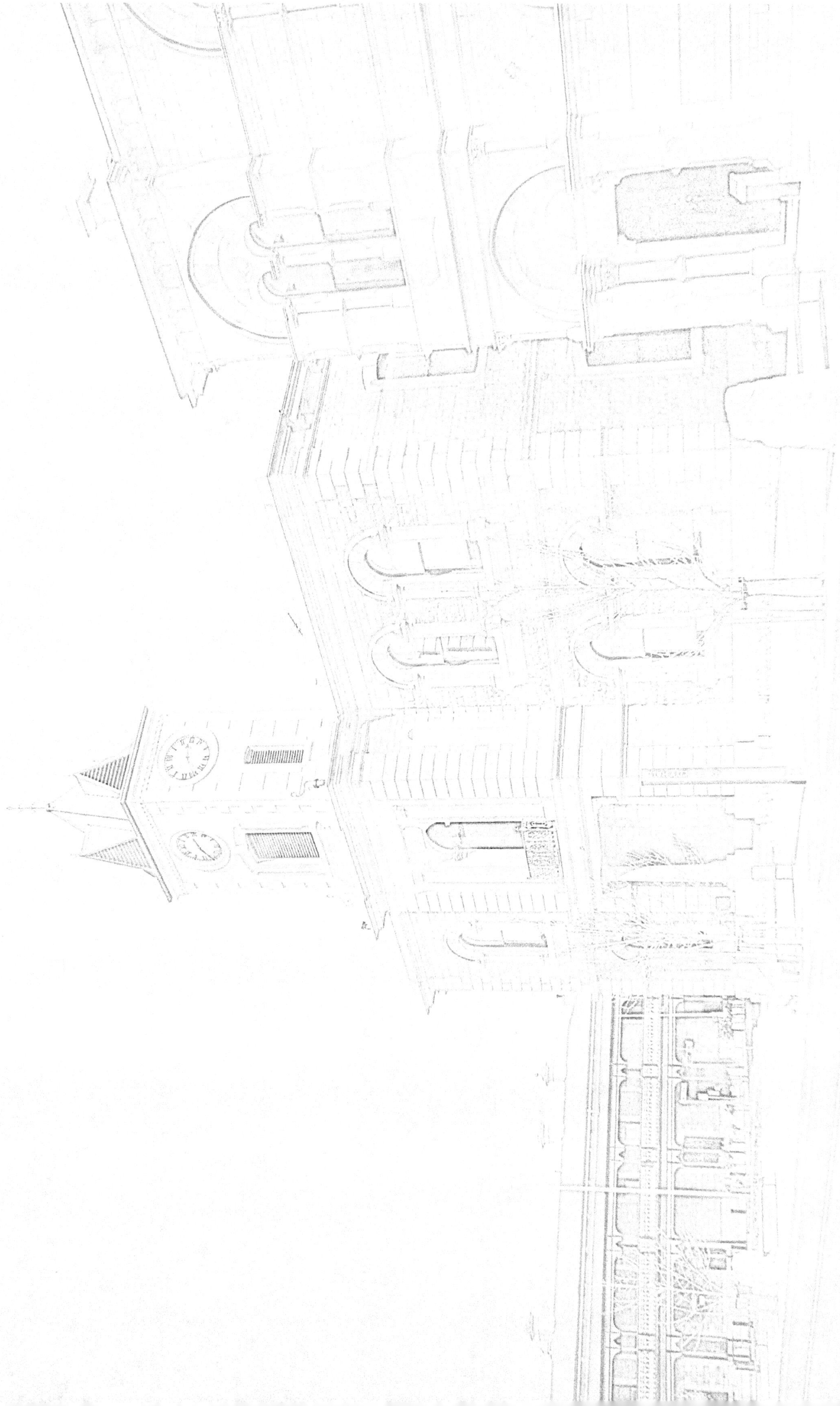

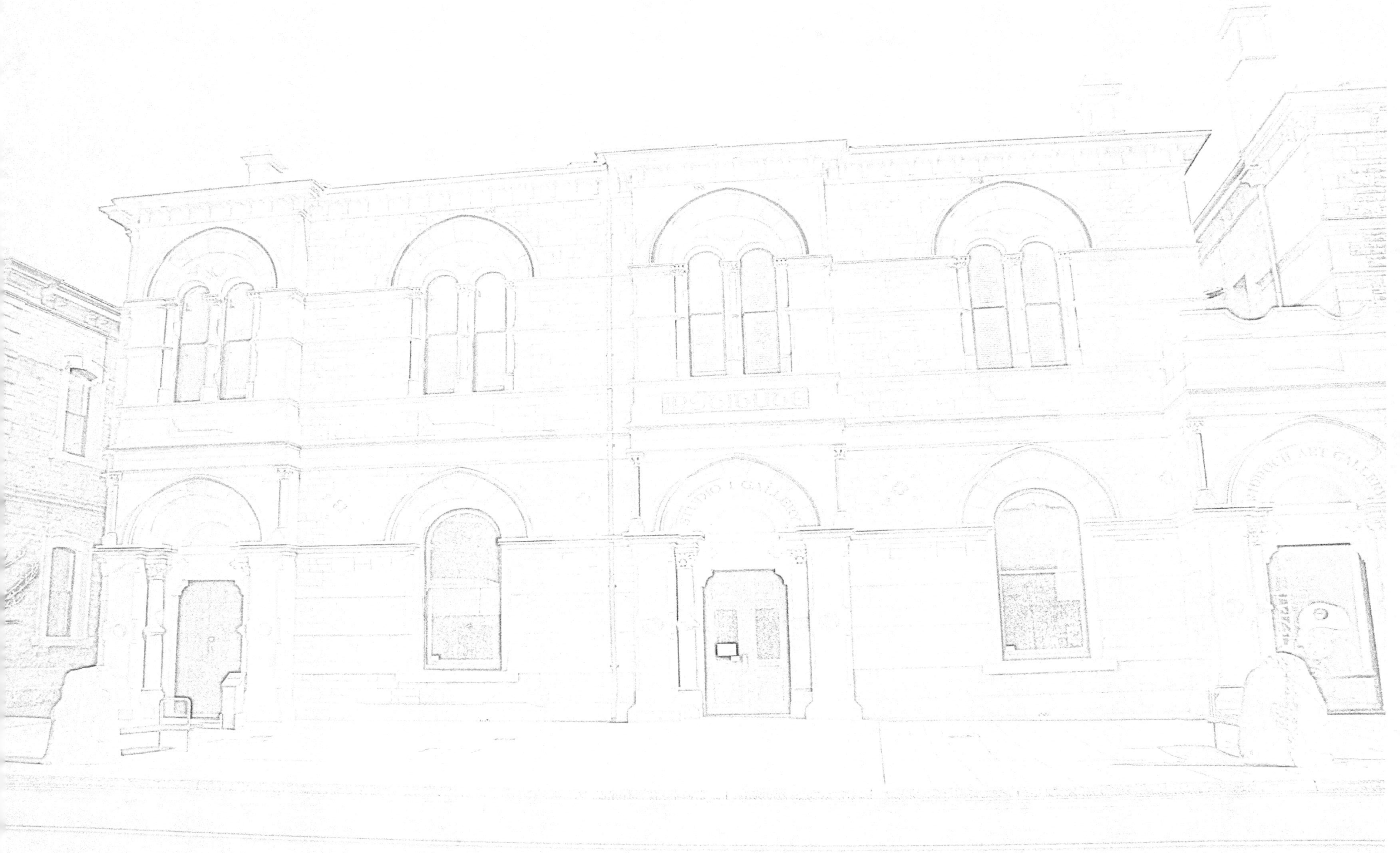
STUDIO 1 GALLERY

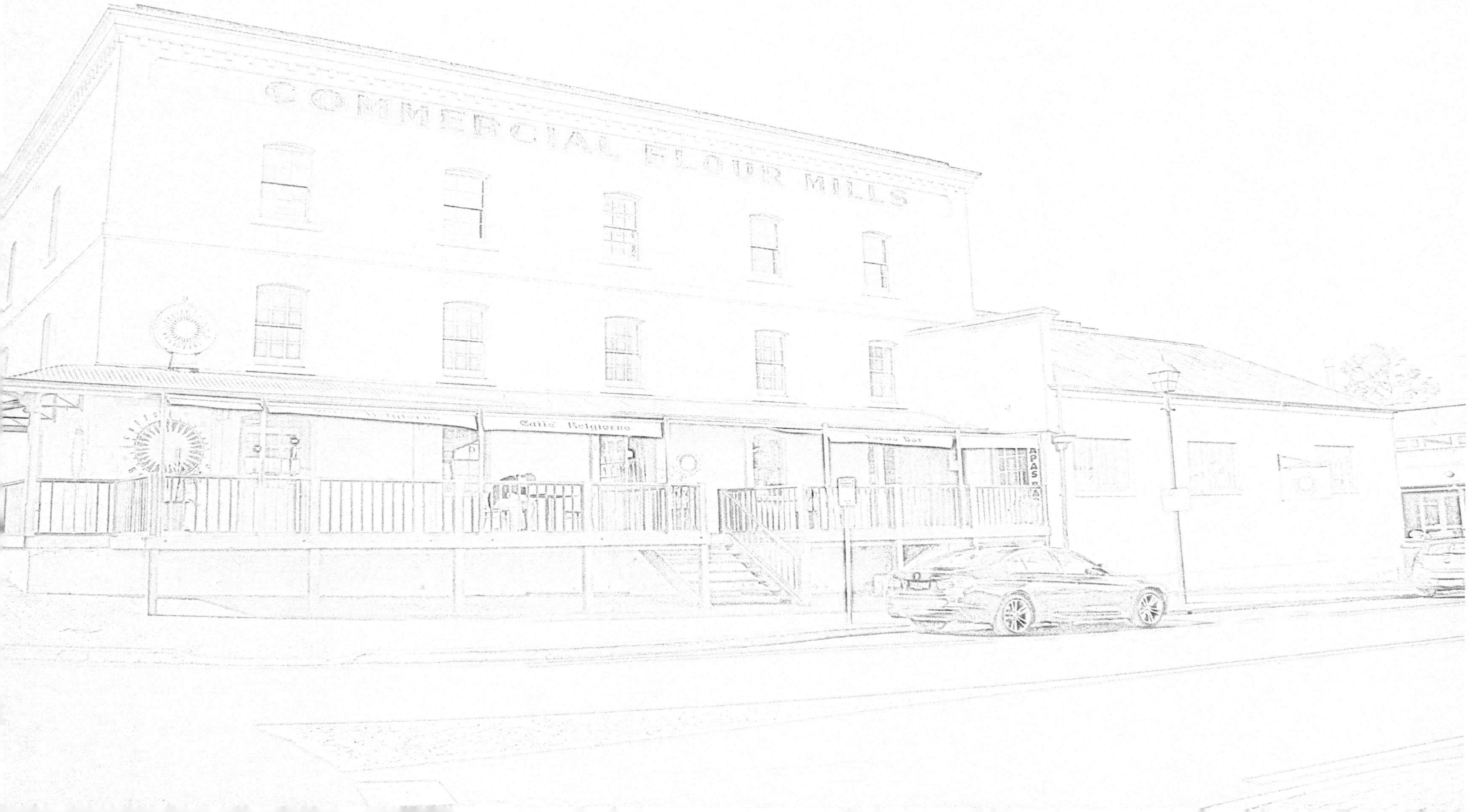
COMMERCIAL FLOUR MILLS
Caffe Belgiorno

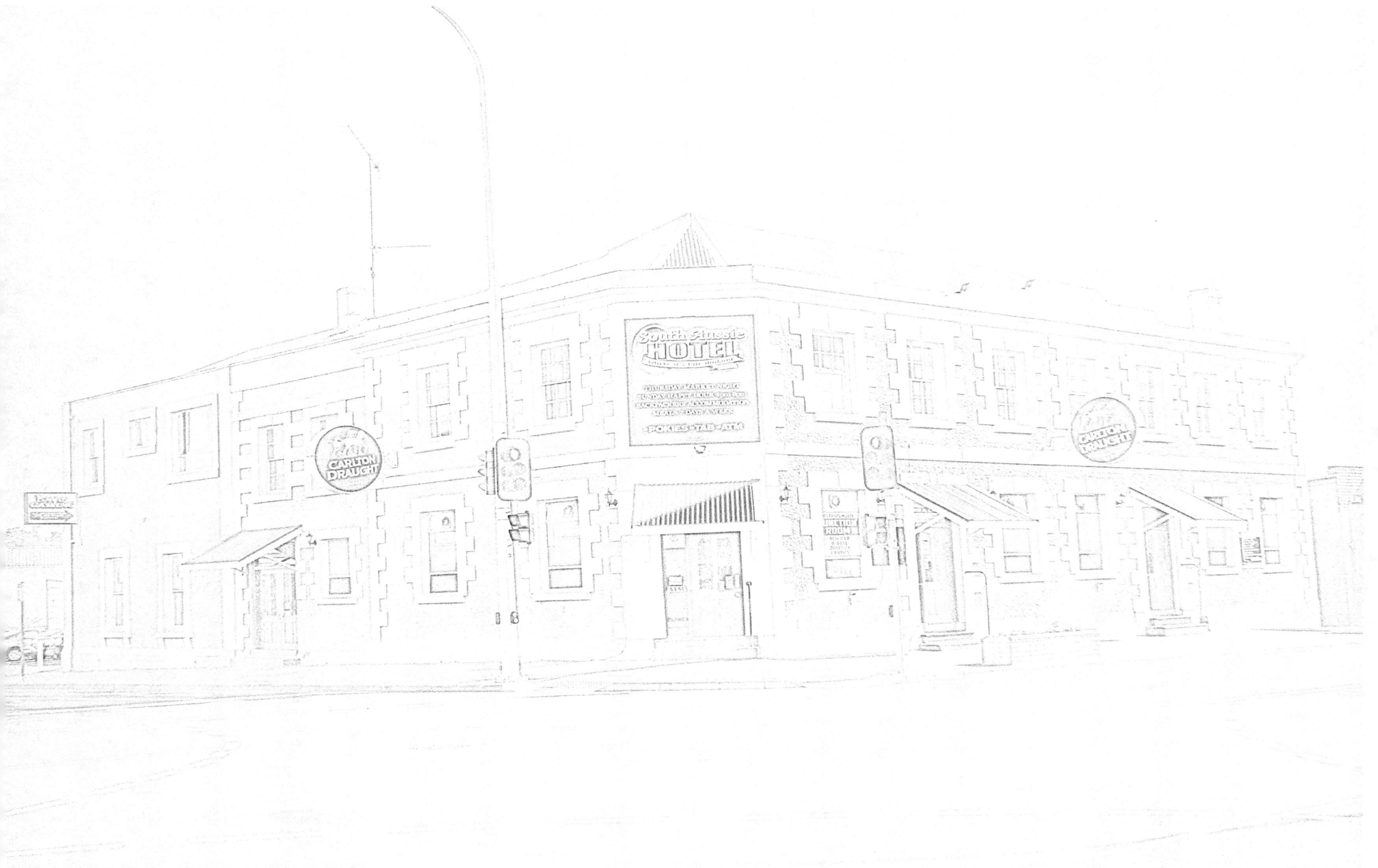
South Aussie
HOTEL
POKIES • TAB • ATM
CARLTON DRAUGHT
CARLTON DRAUGHT

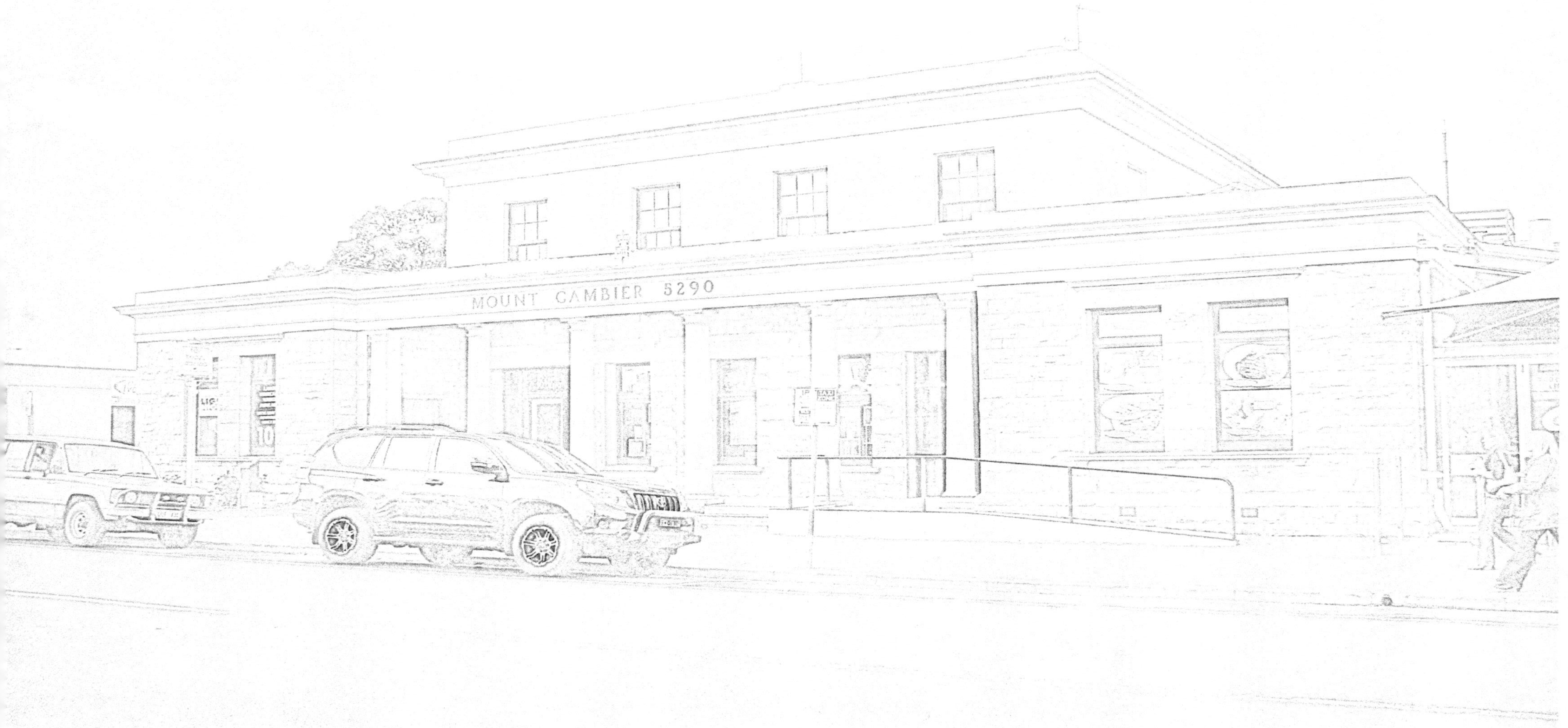
MOUNT GAMBIER 5290

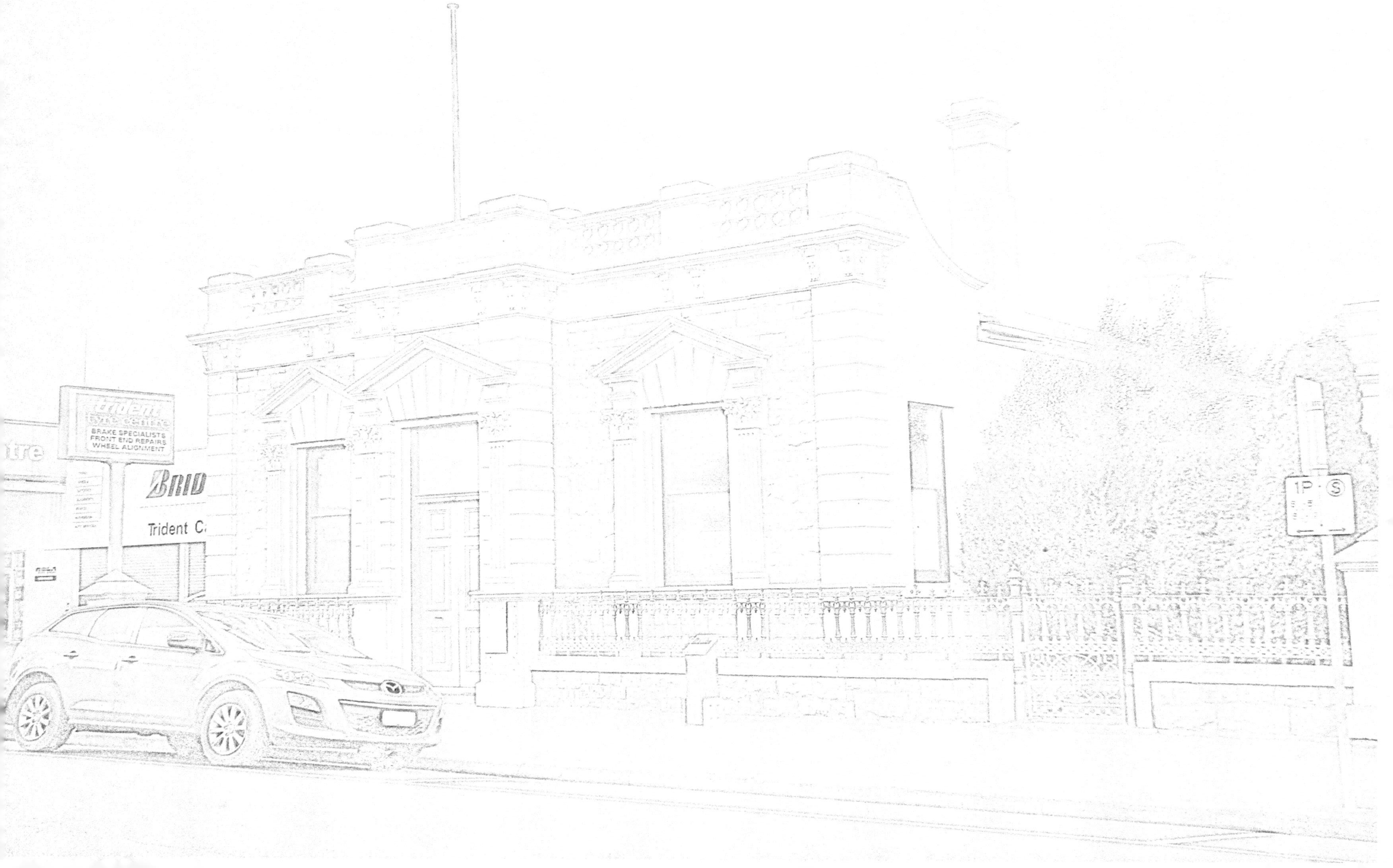
tre
BRAKE SPECIALISTS
FRONT END REPAIRS
WHEEL ALIGNMENT
Trident C
1P

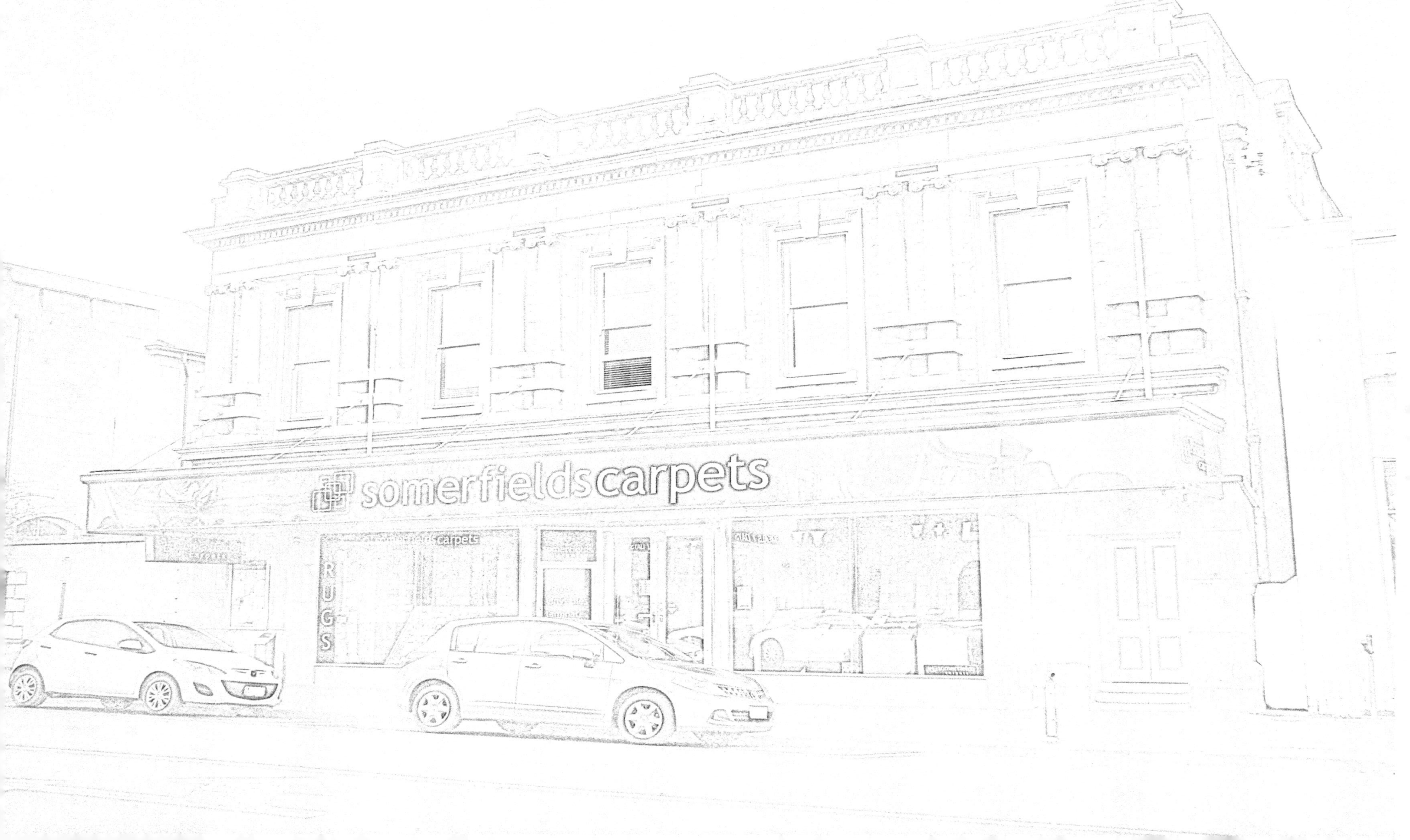
somerfieldscarpets
somerfields carpets
RUGS

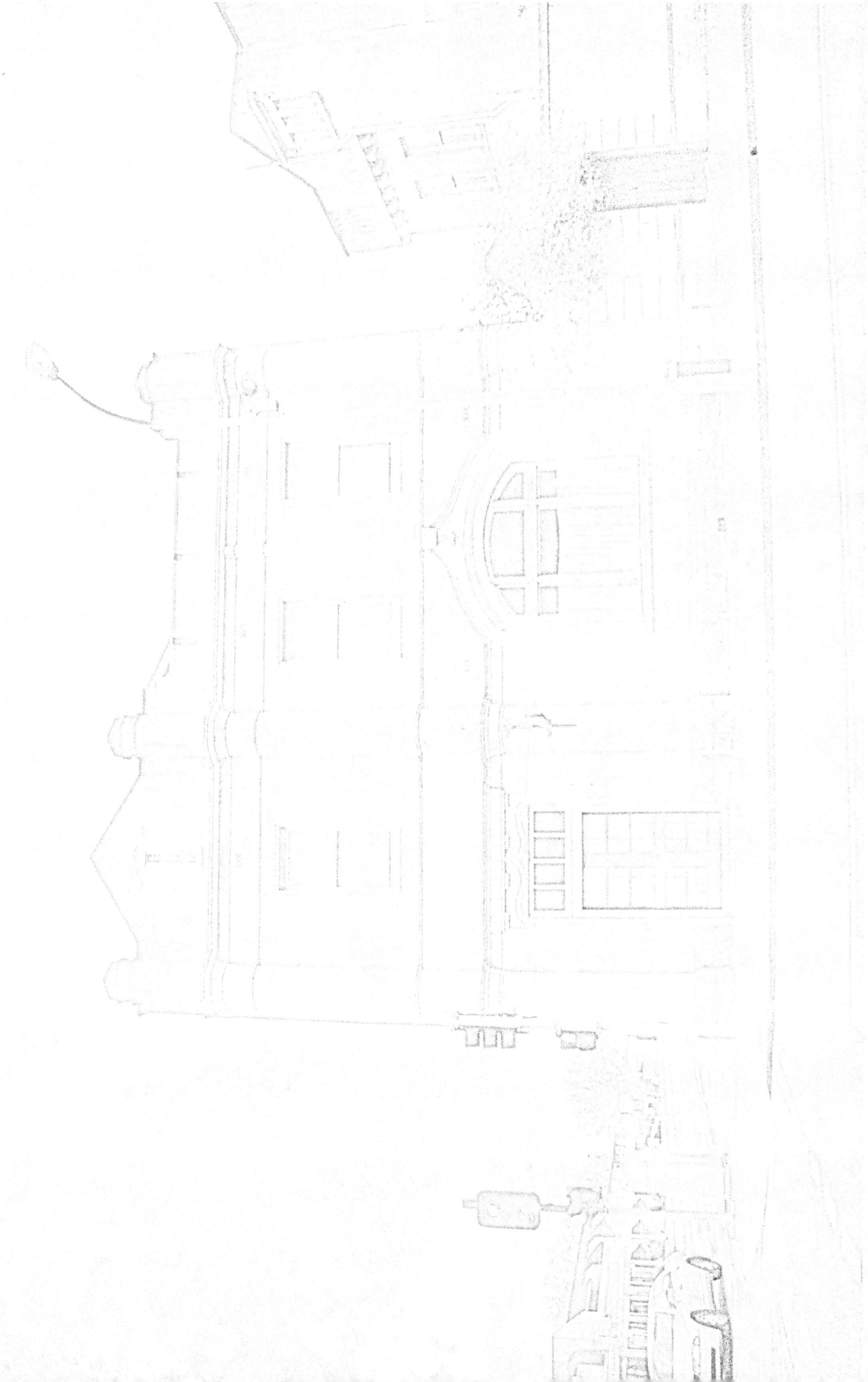

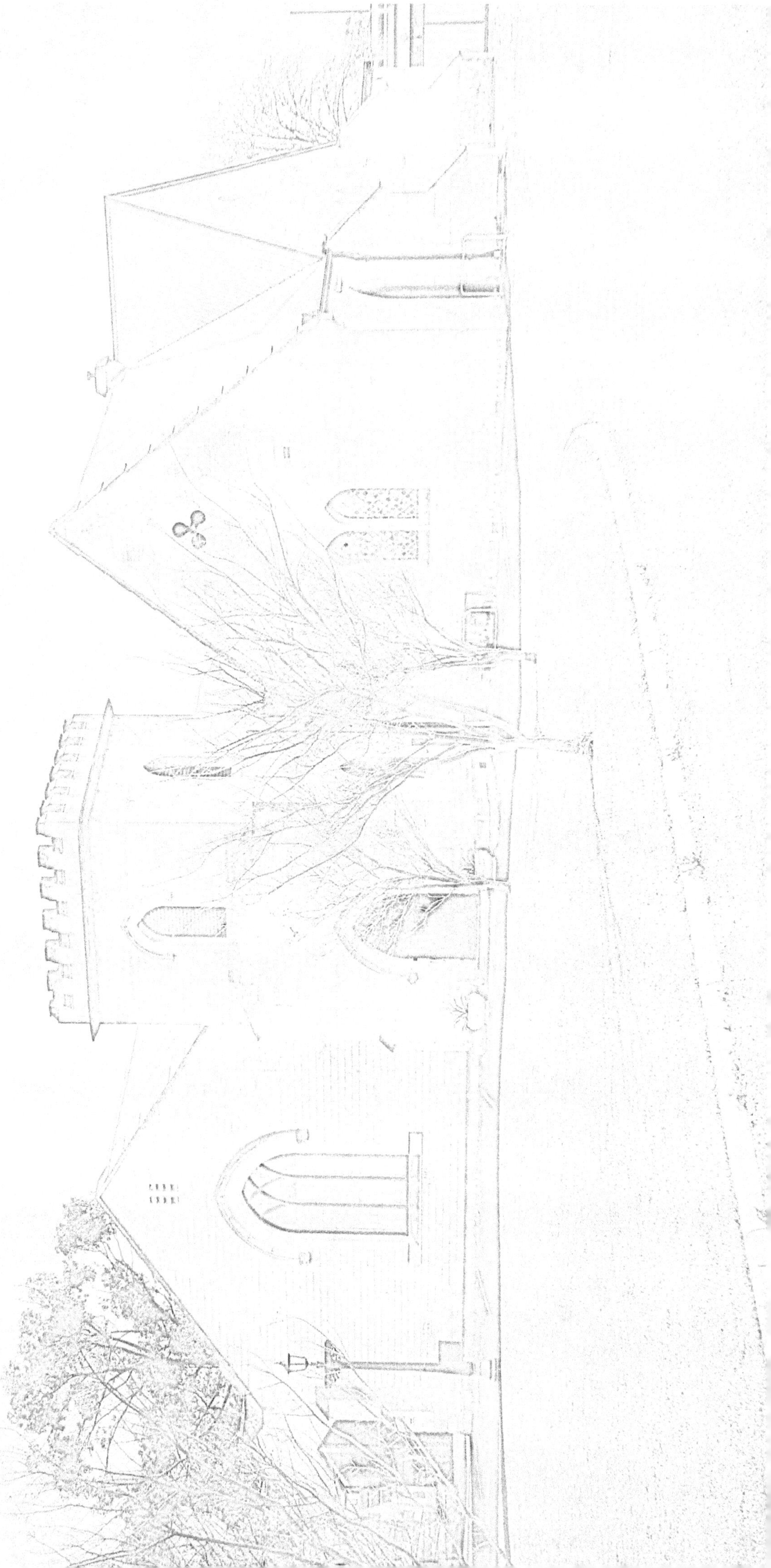

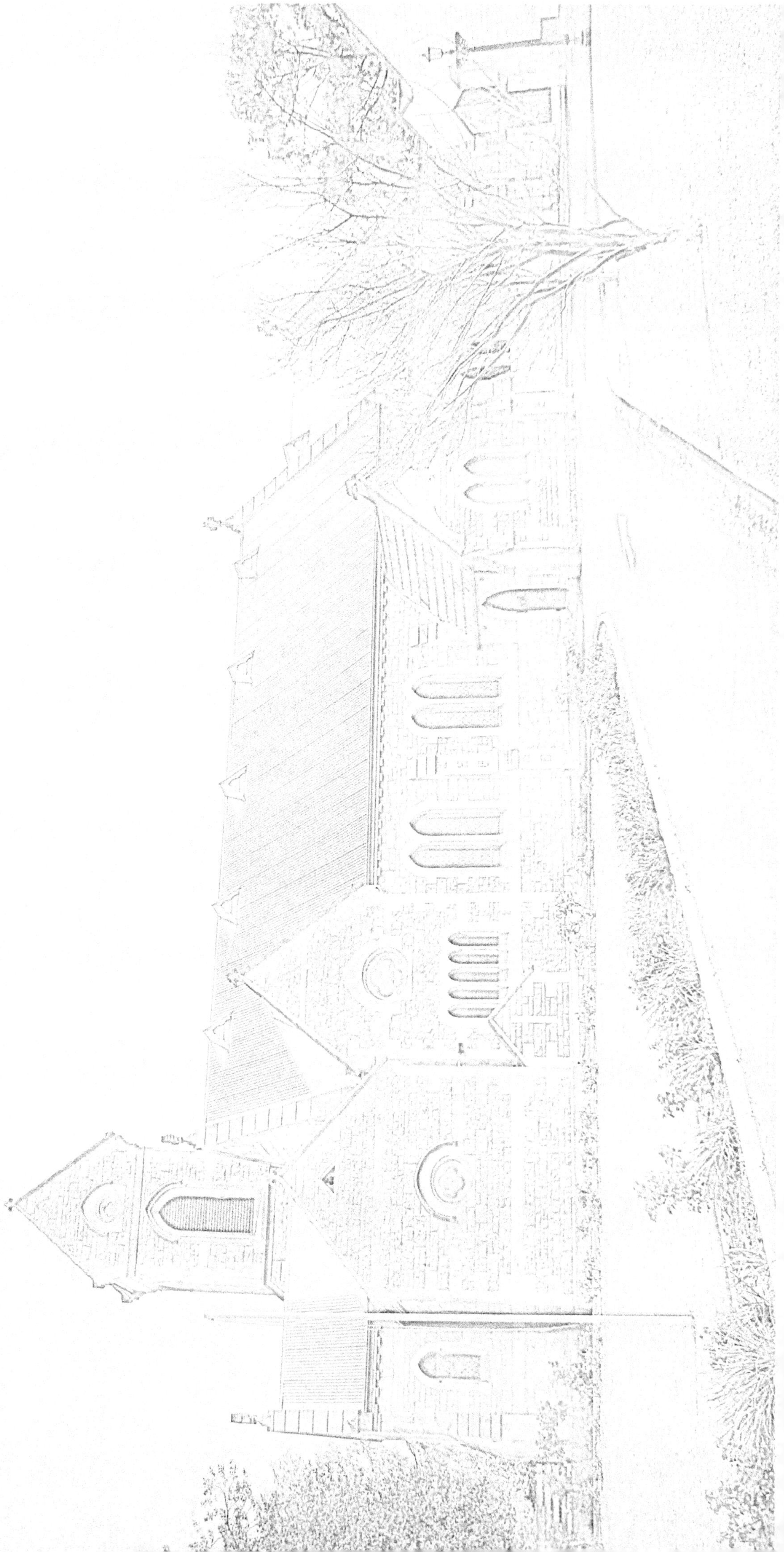

SERVICE TIMES

LIME
LIME

www.ingramcontent.com/pod-product-compliance
Lightning Source LLC
Chambersburg PA
CBHW081059180526
45170CB00005B/1816